The Paris Commune

Reinventions of the Paris Commune
Edited by Kristin Ross

Available titles in the series:

The Paris Commune

~

A Brief History

CAROLYN J. EICHNER

Rutgers University Press

New Brunswick, Camden, and Newark, New Jersey, and London

Library of Congress Cataloging-in-Publication Data

Names: Eichner, Carolyn Jeanne, 1961- author.
Title: The Paris Commune : a brief history / Carolyn J. Eichner.
Description: New Brunswick : Rutgers University Press, [2022] | Series: Reinventions
of the Paris Commune | Includes bibliographical references and index.
Identifiers: LCCN 2021025109 | ISBN 9781978827684 (paperback) |
ISBN 9781978827691 (hardcover) | ISBN 9781978827707 (epub) |
ISBN 9781978827714 (pdf)
Subjects: LCSH: Paris (France)—History—Commune, 1871. |
Women revolutionaries—France—Paris—History—19th century. |
Revolutionaries—France—Paris—History—19th century. | Revolutions
and socialism—France—History—19th century.
Classification: LCC DC316 .E43 2022 | DDC 944.081/2—dc23
LC record available at https://lccn.loc.gov/2021025109

A British Cataloging-in-Publication record for this book is available
from the British Library.

References to internet websites (URLs) were accurate at the time of writing.
Neither the author nor Rutgers University Press is responsible for URLs that may
have expired or changed since the manuscript was prepared.

♾ The paper used in this publication meets the requirements of the
American National Standard for Information Sciences—Permanence of
Paper for Printed Library Materials, ANSI Z39.48-1992.

www.rutgersuniversitypress.org

Printed and bound by CPI Group (UK) Ltd, Croydon, CR0 4YY

For Kennan

Contents

The Paris Commune

1
Illumination

Nearly ten thousand people crowded into the Tuileries Palace on Sunday afternoon, May 21, 1871, for a grand concert benefiting the battlefield hospitals of the revolutionary civil war known as the Paris Commune. Entering through gardens illuminated by red lanterns woven through the trees, attendees arrived in opulent rooms, "upholstered in crimson velvet accented with golden screens." The audience waited to experience the widely advertised extravaganza of "orations, singing, and perhaps dancing" by Paris's top performers, who shared the stage with 1,500 musicians.[1] Louis Barron, a twenty-four-year-old member of the Commune government, observed that rather than the usual aristocratic spectators, the "crystal chandelier blazing from the ceiling" illuminated a crowd that included working women and men, people "who seemed to say, 'Finally, we are in our house, in our palace! We have driven out the tyrant, and we can now use this place as we please!'"[2] Awaiting the performance, the Communard journalist Maxime Vuillaume observed "a long, long table. Hundreds of glasses, bottles . . . mountains of brioche," a rich abundance for all to share.[3] Vuillaume felt "a buzz of impatience" run through the crowd until, finally, "The curtain rose. Silence. On the stage, a strong woman . . . La Bordas." Revolutionary red belt around her waist, the renowned performer began to sing "*La Canaille*"—"The Rabble"—the working-class anthem for which she was famous. Her voice unleashed the story of the common people, "their sons born on straw, have only a slum for a palace." Yet now *la canaille* filled the lavish rooms of France's Tuileries Palace. "It is the honest man," La Bordas continued singing, "whose hand, by the pen or hammer, pays with sweat for his bit of bread." Mid-song, a Parisian National Guardsman, a member of the Commune's army, strode onstage and "handed the artist a flag . . . which she slowly unfurled . . . and wrapped herself in. . . . She continued to sing. And it was a gripping spectacle." Holding a dazzling and dramatic festival in the tradition of the great French Revolution, the Commune government welcomed all Parisians to the once-royal residence, now resplendent with the red flag of revolution.

This spectacular palace concert embodied the inclusive and liberatory politics of the Paris Commune. Rejoicing in the triumph of the people of Paris, who had taken control of their city and cast off the repressive French national government, the concert represented a new society under a municipal government directly responsible to its citizens. It celebrated the collective experiment toward erasing class and gender inequalities, the end of labor abuses and exploitations, the elimination of the oppressive police force, the democratization of education and the arts, and the creation of a revolutionary sense of community. The Commune had flung open the Tuileries Palace doors to the people of Paris. In this once-elite space, the formerly excluded citizens basked in the art, music, abundance, and liberty long denied them.

At the same moment, on the afternoon of May 21, the French National Army slipped through an unguarded section of Paris's city walls, aiming for not only military conquest but also mass slaughter of Parisians. When the uprising had begun two months earlier, the French national government had abandoned Paris for Versailles, the old royal city. On May 21, a Versailles sympathizer named Jules Ducatel saw the Point-du-Jour gate left unprotected. He scaled the wall and waved a white handkerchief to signal the government troops stationed just outside. Naval Captain Auguste Trève saw the sign, investigated, determined that the gate was indeed undefended, and marched the first National Army soldiers into Paris. Behind them, the 130,000 troops that had held Paris under siege for two months readied to inundate the city.[4] They had a single goal: to destroy the Commune. Adolphe Thiers, head of the French government, had sworn at the beginning of the conflict to "defend order." In his eyes, and those of most of the national government, the military, the bourgeoisie, the peasantry, and the Catholic Church, the Commune embodied the antithesis of order. The uprising's toppling of hierarchies and its attempts to radically re-create relations of power and authority, profoundly angered and frightened those defenders of order and the status quo. While the army's loyalties were many—to the state, to religion, to capitalism, and to the traditional family—its unified aim was to definitively reassert French authority over Paris. The Communards' takeover of the capital, and the subsequent months of revolutionary civil war, had exponentially intensified the wrath that Thiers and the "forces of order" felt toward the insurgents, people who actively worked to undermine their dominance. To this end, the army hurtled into Paris on May 21. From generals to infantry ranks, they intended to show no mercy to the revolutionaries.

One week later, the Tuileries Palace smoldered in ashes, and across the city as many as 15,000 to 20,000 Parisians lay dead. In what became known as the "Bloody Week," Communard men and women battled the army in the streets, behind barricades built by ripping up paving stones and heaping horse carts, furniture, barrels, window frames, books, and anything else at hand, attempting to defend their egalitarian society. The Bloody Week saw the Versailles government, in the name of "order," use overwhelming force not only to extinguish the Commune and all it represented, but also to exterminate the people who had built it. Infantry and cavalry of all ranks ruthlessly attacked Parisian men, women, and children, leaving "mountains of cadavers" in the streets,[5] assaulting citizens as they would "wild beasts, ferocious . . . sinister enemies of France," as army officer Eugène Hennebert described Communards.[6] Communard Louise Michel reported, "The machine guns roared . . . they killed as in a hunt; it was a human butchery."[7] The French National Army became the first military force to use machine guns for mass executions. And they used them on their own citizens. In the fighting, the Tuileries Palace, the Hôtel de Ville (City Hall), the Prefecture of Police (police headquarters), and the Law Courts went up in flames.

Versailles blamed working-class women for starting the fires, reacting against the significant feminist activism during the Commune.[8] This justified shooting any suspicious-looking woman or child (considered accomplices); merely a working-class appearance qualified one as suspicious. Some of the captured Communard women and men faced immediate execution, while thousands of others experienced arrest, "battlefield" court-martial, summary trials, and firing squads. The Paris correspondent of the *London Standard* newspaper reported, "The wholesale executions continue indiscriminately. . . . At one of these, since last night five hundred persons have been shot. . . . There are invariably women and boys among them. . . . Prisoners are soon disposed of by a volley and tumbled into a trench, when, if not killed by the shots, death from suffocation must soon put an end to their pain."[9]

The French military and political authorities did nothing to stop the slaughter. The "forces of order" intended not only to decimate the revolution and the revolutionaries, but also to make clear that radical activism—socialism, anarchism, labor movements, and feminism—could and would be crushed. Aware of the eyes of the world on them, Thiers and his government hoped to unambiguously demonstrate the brutal fate awaiting anyone attempting to rise up against the power of the state.

The Paris Commune was the French revolutionary civil war that rocked the nineteenth century and shaped the twentieth. Considered a golden moment of hope and potential by the left, and a black hour of terrifying power inversions by the right, the Commune occupies a critical position in understanding modern history and politics. A seventy-two-day conflict that ended with the ferocious slaughter of Parisians, the Commune represents for some the final insurgent burst of the French Revolution's long wake, for others the first "successful" socialist uprising, and for yet others an archetype for egalitarian socioeconomic and political change. The Commune looms large in histories of France, nineteenth-century

Europe, twentieth-century revolutions, and civil wars, as well as socialism, anarchism, and feminism. Militants have referenced and incorporated its ideas into insurrections across the globe, throughout the twentieth and into the twenty-first centuries, keeping alive the revolution's now-iconic goals and images. Innumerable scholars in countless languages have examined aspects of the 1871 uprising, taking perspectives ranging from glorifying to damning this world-shaking event.

The Commune stands as a critical and pivotal moment in nineteenth-century history, as the linchpin between revolutionary pasts and futures, and as the crucible allowing glimpses of alternate possibilities. Upending hierarchies of class, religion, and gender, the Commune emerged as a touchstone for the subsequent century and a half of revolutionary and radical social movements.

Sparks: The City

During France's Second Empire, the authoritarian period prior to the Commune, Louis-Napoléon Bonaparte (Napoléon III, the nephew of Napoléon Bonaparte) ruled from the time of his 1851 coup d'état until his 1870 capture on the battlefield during the ill-fated Franco-Prussian War. His rule saw economic prosperity and a suppression of most political opposition, making him popular with the elites and the peasantry.

France had five predominant socioeconomic groups during this period. The aristocracy, the traditional elites typically linked to the monarchy, held inherited titles and wealth, often reaching back before the Revolution of 1789. The bourgeoisie, the more recent wealthy class of factory owners, lawyers, and "bosses," generally advocated capitalism. Small shopkeepers and skilled artisans, the petite bourgeoisie, made up the next level. Below them, the working class comprised the majority of the urban population, including people who earned their living doing manual, industrial, and some artisanal labor. In the countryside and villages, the peasantry constituted the final group, consisting mostly of small farmers and agricultural laborers. Holding particular and often conflicting interests, these five groups, or classes, tended to resent or fear each other. Power in France relied on shifting alliances among them. Seeking to modernize and beautify crowded, centuries-old Paris, Louis-Napoléon physically reshaped the city. Demolishing warrens of tight, medieval-era streets and neighborhoods, he replaced them with the open, sweeping boulevards of today's Paris. Fear of social unrest also fueled this grand reconstruction. In the 1790s, 1830, 1848, and 1851, revolutionary Parisians had built street barricades to block and battle troops. Recognizing that working-class Parisians could retake the city by thus obstructing the streets, the Second Empire intended the new, expansive avenues both to prevent barricading and to facilitate unimpeded military movement. Razing dense districts also meant dislocating the urban poor by demolishing their homes and constructing high-priced properties in their place. This redevelopment pushed workers to the Parisian periphery. Only recently incorporated into the city, these undeveloped areas, including Montmartre, Belleville, and La Villette in the north and northeast, and Montparnasse and Batignolles in the south, would become cradles of insurrection.

Its history saturated in revolution, Paris loomed as an insurgent specter over decades of French national leadership. Parisian events had led to France's seven governmental changes between the French Revolution in 1789 and the 1851 birth of the Second Empire. Even earlier, as historian Frank Jellinek explained, "The ruler of France had, historically, been a hostage in Paris."[10] French kings had contended with significant social unrest for centuries, reaching back to Parisian Mayor Etienne Marcel expelling the monarch and establishing an autonomous Commune of Paris in 1357.[11] (The word "Commune," in both fourteenth- and nineteenth-century contexts, meant municipality.) As a result of this history, in 1795 Paris had lost the right to rule itself. Frightened of the insurgent tendencies of the city's multiple radical undercurrents, the national government continued to deny Paris an elected mayor and municipal autonomy for nearly two hundred years, until 1975. The fight for self-rule undergirded many Parisian movements over these centuries.

The capital stood in long-term opposition to the provinces. Both the rural peasantry and the provincial aristocracy, conservative in manners and politics, resented Paris and its inhabitants. Hostile to its concentration of wealth, its cosmopolitanism, urbanism, and attraction to rural youth, the mostly agrarian provincial population also disdained the capital's radical tradition. Resentments flowed both ways, as most Parisians considered the provinces reactionary deadweight holding back French progress. Peasants and rural aristocrats generally either supported the authoritarian Emperor Louis-Napoléon or advocated the restoration of the monarchy, with the latter increasing as the former's popularity waned into the 1860s. Simultaneously in Paris, opposition politics struggled to resurface, following nearly two decades of suppression. Most Parisian activists ignored the peasantry or considered them unalterably regressive. The future Communards André Léo (pseudonym of Léodile Béra Champseix), a socialist feminist female novelist and journalist, and Elisée Reclus, an anarchist feminist male writer and renowned geographer, did not. Proposing a rural propaganda campaign, they wrote in 1869, "we must turn all of our democratic efforts toward the countryside," which up to then had been "so fatal to the honor and true prosperity of the country."[12] Their historically informed warnings against the dangers of provincial reaction went unheeded. The anti-Parisian resentments would resurface violently in the primarily peasant Versailles army during the Commune.

Sparks: Politics

The Second Empire had crushed the short-lived Second Republic (1848–1851), but not the ideals of republicanism. A decade and a half later, republicans made up a notable portion of the opposition to the Second Empire. Republicanism held that the will of the people rested in legislatures and laws, concepts they traced back to the 1789 French Revolution's founding ideas of liberty, equality, and fraternity. Yet republicanism itself, as a foundational concept, was divided between reactionary, liberal bourgeois, and socialist or radical strains. While conservative republicanism asserted limited representation and restricted rights and freedoms, the liberal form sought a more egalitarian political democracy. Republican socialism—the third and most expansive form of republicanism—not only promoted political equality but also addressed economic and social injustices. Profound differences fueled conflict among the factions.

Within each group, however, the vast majority of adherents only recognized 50 percent of the population as eligible for rights: the male half. In response, republican liberal feminists and republican socialist feminists advocated democratic forms in which men and women enjoyed equal rights and freedoms.

France's Napoleonic Civil Code of Law, in place since the beginning of the nineteenth century, denied citizenship to women. It consigned adult women to the status of a minor child, initially under the authority of their fathers and then under the control of their husbands. Even though they held adult responsibility for crimes committed, they had neither political nor juridical rights. The Civil Code clearly stated: "The people deprived of juridical rights are minors, married women, criminals, and the mentally debilitated." Moreover, marriage legally subsumed women to their husbands. "The husband owes protection to his wife, the wife obedience to her husband"; it gave the husband control over her wages, property, and legal affairs. A husband could legally kill his wife if he discovered her with her lover; if a wife slayed her husband under similar circumstances, she would face murder charges.[13] Feminists contested these gender-based legal marginalizations and subjugations from the imposition of the Civil Code.

Feminist politics wove through the nineteenth century and directly influenced the emergence and development of the Commune. French feminisms arose from two different phases of the French Revolution: 1789's liberalism and 1793's radicalism. The liberal strand of feminism, which evolved into republican liberal feminism and republican socialist feminism, sought women's suffrage and equal rights under law. In contrast, the more radical branch developed into anarchist and revolutionary socialist feminisms,

1.1. Marie Ferré, Louise Michel, and Paule Mink. Courtesy of The Charles Deering McCormick Library of University Archives and Special Collections, Northwestern University.

both of which sought the overthrow of existing governmental systems. In 1866, future Communards André Léo, Louise Michel, and Paule Mink joined with feminists across the republican spectrum, organizing La Société du Droit des Femmes, "The Society for Women's Rights," to promote women's equality under the law.[14] In 1868, Léo elaborated and theorized her position regarding the denial of women's rights. Her widely republished and highly debated "Manifesto" avowed "no justice and no peace will exist in the world until the gravest of social inequities will be eradicated."[15] In it Léo demanded women's inclusion in the three central tenets of French republicanism: liberty, equality, and fraternity. With the advent of the 1871 revolutionary insurgency, however, all three women abandoned rights-based republicanism, working instead toward egalitarian socialist and anarchist change. The liberatory visions of these politics incubated during the late Empire, expanding and exploding across Paris during the Commune.

Near the Empire's end, Louis-Napoléon attempted to counter his waning popularity by easing (but not fully removing) restrictions on the press, speech, and assembly. Striving to appear as a populist emperor, he hoped to win the allegiance of the working classes. In response to this 1868 expansion of freedoms, activists and thinkers—long silenced by the Second Empire's repressions— opened discussions and debates. Republicans, socialists, feminists, and workers were suddenly able to somewhat openly express political discontent and opposition for the first time in nearly two decades. Newspapers proliferated, debates raged.

Sparks: Public Meetings

These discussions had a profoundly collective dimension: public meetings sprang up throughout Paris. Attracting thousands of people to venues across the city, public meetings (*réunions publiques*) served as places to express grievances and to deliberate political issues. "Women's Work," "Capital and Interest," and "Marriage and Divorce" made up some of the many announced meeting topics. Deliberating and hearing various opinions politicized and radicalized numerous women and men. Speakers challenged multiple aspects of what, at an October 1869 meeting, the socialist bookbinder and future Communard Eugène Varlin termed a "worm-eaten society."[16] The gatherings addressed issues and structures that shaped Parisians' lives, drawing people from the range of groups opposed to Louis-Napoléon's government. While many of the lecturers were activists like Léo and Varlin, the openness and democratic nature of the assemblies allowed working-class women and men to step up to podiums and express their own concerns, anger, and desires. As Léo wrote in the newspaper *L'Opinion nationale*, only weeks after the meetings began, "working women with fingers bruised from toiling all day, listen and learn. . . . Several of them . . . also want to speak."[17] Parisians thus created a public sphere for ideas, one driven by and attentive to the lives of workers.

Many of the lectures focused on economic questions. In October 1869, a speaker identified as "Madame Pirée" attacked capitalists and the bourgeoisie, denouncing long-standing inequities and class resentments. Paule Mink declared, "Accumulated capital is unjust."[18] Orators at other events condemned the power and influence of the Catholic Church, indicative of the strong strain of anticlericalism among the era's leftists and working class. An anonymous speaker at the Salle Robert accused priests of "abusing the influence that confession gives them to seduce the daughters of workers," while André Léo insisted that the Church's control over education exposed children to "illogic and superstition."[19] Moving beyond a specific focus on the Catholic Church, *citoyen* (citizen) Pichon indicted religion more broadly, characterizing it as "the essential cause of wars, murders, and plunder."[20] In some lectures, female and male feminists and like-minded thinkers contested the authoritarianism of patriarchy in both the family and the state. Lawyer, journalist, and future Communard Abel Peyrouton decried "the dangerous authority transmitted directly from the head of the family to the head of the state,"[21] while Madame Désirée called for "the recognition of the equality of man and woman,"[22] and Mademoiselle Brugerolles declared that "women must throw off men's chains."[23]

The *réunions publiques* presented the opportunity to share common concerns, experiences, and objectives. An emergent class consciousness, and with it a sense of solidarity, enabled working-class Parisians both to imagine the possibility of a more egalitarian world and to envision their own role in bringing it about. The number of meetings varied each night, and attendance fluctuated significantly depending on the subject, location, and date. Sessions near election days drew the largest crowds. Two years before the Commune, on March 3, 1869, seven meetings together attracted between ten and fifteen thousand participants; the fourteen events on May 11 involved twenty thousand attendees; and, according to Paris police reports, on May 12 twenty-three thousand people filled eighteen sessions, while an overflow of nearly another fifty thousand spilled into the streets.[24] Extensive, substantive, and influential, the public meetings served as training grounds for popular involvement in the revolutionary political clubs that emerged during the Commune.

Sparks: The International

Issues of exploitative labor practices also found substantial traction in these assemblies, drawing in the city's artisans and workers. The International Workingmen's Association (IWA) dominated the late Empire's labor and socialist scenes. Formed by French and British delegates in London in 1864, the IWA (also known as the First International) brought together a broad range of leftist organizations, seeking international solidarity among socialists and workers. A significant number of future Communards became members of the Parisian branch of the International, despite persistent oppression from Louis-Napoléon's government, as well as evolving internal conflicts. These included Léo and Varlin.

The grandson of a participant in the 1848 Revolution, Eugène Varlin was born in 1839 to an impoverished provincial family and raised on republican ideals and traditions. Sent to Paris at age fifteen to apprentice as a bookbinder, he joined the ranks of the city's "labor aristocracy" as a practitioner of this specialized craft.

Such skilled laborers, in trades including saddlery, locksmithing, and bronze work, played significant roles in the Parisian labor movement. Beginning his activism in the late 1850s, Varlin participated in the push to reduce the workday to ten hours. Involved in the bookbinders' strikes of 1864–1865 and in establishing the bookbinders' union and the Parisian Federation of Workers' Societies, he also started a Mutual Credit Society for the bookbinders' union, for which he faced arrest. Varlin's focus on cooperation among workers extended across national boundaries in his central role in the Parisian branch of the International—activism that resulted in additional time behind bars. Deeply interested in education, Varlin recognized the weakness of his own rural schooling and took advantage of the workers' night classes that emerged in Paris in the 1860s. He augmented his courses by reading the philosopher Jean-Jacques Rousseau and the socialist Louis Blanc. In turn, he advocated improvements in education for workers, peasants, and girls, participating in the founding of a girls' school in 1869.[25]

Varlin held strong feminist convictions, a stance that conflicted with other male socialists of the era. Most members of the Parisian section of the International followed the anarchist theorist Pierre-Joseph Proudhon. An advocate of radical liberty—he supported labor organizing but rejected strikes and political action as undercutting individual freedom—Proudhon also opposed women's labor participation and women's liberty. Insisting on women's fundamental incapacity and inferiority, Proudhon developed a calculus to "prove" that "Inferior to man in conscience as much as in intellectual and muscular power, woman finds herself . . . definitively relegated to the second rank. . . . Her comparative value remains 2 to 3."[26] In pointed contrast to the Proudhonians, Varlin wrote the statutes of the bookbinders' union to assure that "women will be equally admitted to the association and will play the same role as men," and underscored the organization's gender equity in naming it the Société des Relieurs et Relieuses, the "Society of Men and Women Bookbinders."[27] Working with fellow bookbinder, International member, feminist, and future Communard Nathalie Lemel, in 1866 Varlin started a food cooperative, La Marmite ("The

Pot") which supported workers beyond the end of the Empire and throughout the Commune. At the Geneva, Switzerland, meeting of the International that same year, Varlin called for equal pay for equal work for women and men, stating, "her needs are as great as ours, she must be rewarded as we are . . . same product, same salary."[28] His proposal failed.[29]

The Proudhonian domination of the Paris International waned by the decade's end, as the association expanded to include other branches of socialism. These included followers of the conspiratorial revolutionary socialist Louis-Auguste Blanqui, a faction constituting a significant portion of the anti-Bonaparte opposition. Rather than adopting the republican ideals of 1789, these socialists championed the Jacobin legacy of 1793, the most radical year of the French Revolution. Uninterested in organizing the working class, they instead adopted a more top-down, highly secretive, less collective approach to socialism. They pushed political and confrontational stances. These internal conflicts within the International during the 1860s prefigured some of those that would plague the Commune, including questions of women's involvement and women's roles.

André Léo participated in the International, along with several other future Communard women including Mink, Lemel, and the Russian Elisabeth Dmitrieff. Born into a provincial bourgeois family in 1824, Léo grew up in a book-filled house, studying English and law with her progressive father. Although she was an adult during the Revolution of 1848, historians have little evidence of her life during those cataclysmic years. In 1853, she and her husband, socialist Grègoire Champseix, had twin sons whom they named André and Léo—the source of her distinctly male pseudonym. During the decades of censorship under the Second Empire, Léo used fiction to subtly convey her social and political critiques, often focusing on gender and class issues. In the late 1860s period of liberalization, she published regularly in a range of socialist newspapers, reported on public meetings for *L'Opinion Nationale,* and wrote and spoke on topics including egalitarian education, radicalizing the peasantry, and elevating and expanding both women's work and women's rights. Widely recognized and prolific in the years before the Commune, Léo published fifteen novels (she would publish another fifteen after 1870), numerous works of political analysis and propaganda, and dozens of journalistic articles.[30] As a writer and orator, a co-organizer of the Society for Women's Rights, and member of the International (which included her editorial position on the association's newspaper, *L'Égalité*), Léo advocated a rights-based socialist feminism. She contended that women could be liberated through gradual legal change. With the advent of revolution, however, Léo further radicalized and changed her position.

The Empire Extinguished

The year 1870 opened with the emperor's cousin, Pierre Bonaparte, dramatically shooting socialist journalist Victor Noir. Noir had come to Bonaparte's home to settle the terms of a duel between Bonaparte and the editor of a newspaper critical of the emperor, but Bonaparte killed him instead. Over 100,000 Parisians attended Noir's funeral—making it the largest demonstration during the Second Empire.[31] Nearly the same number of French troops, on high alert, filled Paris streets, indicating the government's fear of an uprising. The revolutionary Blanquists came armed. The future Communard Louise Michel carried a dagger and dressed as a man, "to avoid bothering, or being bothered," as a woman could be unwelcome in such a male-dominated context.[32] Ultimately the socialist leaders, headed by the future Communard Henri Rochefort, the owner of the widely read newspaper for which Noir wrote, decided not to provoke a conflict. The suddenness of the murder and funeral had not allowed time to establish a plan, and Rochefort recognized the wisdom of honoring the wishes of Louis Noir, who "did not want his brother to have a bloody funeral."[33]

Tensions had intensified in the late 1860s as strikes exploded in France's developing industries. Although artisanal labor still dominated Paris during this period, and the majority of workers toiled in small workshops, French industrialization had accelerated. Working twelve or more hours per day for miserable wages, in harsh, dangerous, and dehumanizing circumstances, laborers across industries increasingly demanded better pay and labor conditions. Factory owners, backed by the state, responded by bringing in military and police forces to crush them. On June 8, 1870, the conservative Parisian newspaper *Le Temps* lamented the extent of the strikes: "This movement is overwhelming us, and we have neither the space nor time to mention all of the incidents."[34] This period of intense strike activity overlapped with Paris's public meetings. At many of these lectures, participants took up collections for the strikers and their families. One speaker, Camille Adam, accused Eugène Schneider, owner of the steel mills of Creusot, of "maintaining despotism and tyranny with the aid of rifles."[35] Schneider also served as vice president of the Corps Législative, the Second Empire's legislative body. Emphasizing the political connection between the factory owners and the government, a Citizen Vertut spoke about the Creusot strike at a public meeting on "Capital and Labor." Declaring "Our fathers of '89 overthrew the Bastille; we must now overthrow the Bastille of hunger and ignorance," the citizen underscored the revolutionary current running through these conflicts.[36]

In July, a politically weakened Louis-Napoléon declared war on Prussia, a disastrous undertaking that would bring down the Second Empire. France immediately faced a series of humiliating military setbacks, and on September 2, the emperor and 100,000 troops surrendered to Prussia. The news of this military defeat arrived in Paris in the predawn hours. People flocked to the city center, urged by the morning newspapers to make their presence felt and insist on the Empire's end. A young republican and future journalist, poet, and Communard, Charles Sutter-Laumann, recalled how first the word that "The emperor has been taken prisoner!" rolled through and shocked the crowd. Soon, however, rumors spread that "the Republic will be proclaimed!" Sutter-Laumann recollected that they believed "we will once again see the wonders of '92! It was as though I was dreaming."[37]

André Léo and Louise Michel joined the crowd on the Place de la Concorde, an enormous open space Michel described as "literally full." Bordering the gardens of the Tuileries Palace, the Place de la Concorde lay across the River Seine from the Palais Bourbon, where the Corps Législative met in emergency session. In deliberating whether to prop up the Empire or declare its death, arguments arose between deputies supporting the Empire and those advocating a republic or a return to monarchy. In the mid-afternoon, a crowd of Parisians invaded the legislature, demanding the republic. Eugène Schneider, the vice president of the Corps Législative and owner of the massive Creusot steel works, had unsuccessfully proposed a provisional government with himself at the head. He suddenly faced a throng of working-class Parisians who drove him out of the Palais Bourbon, shouting "Death to the assassin of Creusot, to the exploiter of workers!"[38] Among the legislators, the choice became clear: the opposition deputy Léon Gambetta proclaimed the republic. Recalling the thrilling moment, Léo effused, "resounding cries burst out around the Palais Bourbon, 'Vive la République!!!' Finally! . . . Finally, we are free!"[39] In the closing lines of her poem "Jail Songs," which commemorated the moment and its revolutionary potential, Michel expressed optimism that the newly dawning republic would be radically progressive: "Red was the rising sun."[40] Like Michel, Sutter-Laumann, and so many among the Parisian left, Léo believed that the republic proclaimed that day was to be a democratic and social republic. They shared what she later termed "the invincible naïveté of those who want and hope."[41]

The Republic Born in Fire

France remained at war with Prussia, despite the dramatic governmental change. Parisian deputies, all republican members of the opposition party prior to the Empire's collapse, formed a provisional Government of National Defense. General Louis-Jules Trochu, the military governor of Paris appointed by the emperor the previous month, became president of the new republic. A temporary ruling body formed mid-war, the Government of National Defense was composed of moderate republicans, with the exception of republican socialist Henri Rochefort (the newspaper publisher who had employed murdered journalist Victor Noir). At its head, Trochu followed the Orleanist Party, which advocated a return to monarchy. Monarchists and republicans allied together to stave off the Prussian encroachment. Yet Adolphe Thiers, the Orleanist Party leader who would lead the French government against the Commune the following year, made clear that this was not their sole motivation. Speaking to a small group of his allies, Thiers argued for supporting the Government of National Defense, "giving them the force they need, first to resist the invading enemy, but also against all the bad passions that swarm and ferment behind them."[42] For Thiers and his fellow monarchists, as well as for the moderate republicans of the new government, the threat posed by the radicalized Parisian working class and the revolutionary parties loomed nearly as large as did that of Prussia's invading armies.

When the war began, Louis-Napoléon had revived the Parisian National Guard to defend the city once the regular military left for the front. The National Guard had a mutable history. Originally a bourgeois citizen militia that emerged following the 1789 fall of the Bastille, the National Guard had formed to protect the middle ground—the liberal revolution—against both the reactionary Old Regime and king on the right and the more radical popular movements of the left.[43] Disbanded with the restoration of the monarchy in 1814, the National Guard reformed during the Revolution of 1848, but this time as a worker-led force. Because of its shift from a militia defending the elite order to one supporting the working classes, Louis-Napoléon terminated the National Guard following his 1851 coup d'état. With the need to defend Paris against the Prussians in 1870, the emperor reluctantly formed sixty bourgeois battalions. Pressure from republicans pushed the government to open the National Guard ranks to all Parisian men; they soon numbered nearly 300,000. Attracted both by the desire to defend their country and by the pay (a small sum, but vital during a period when many lacked work), the Guard constituted both a patriotic line of defense and a site of potential solidarity for an armed working class. Both the imperial government and the subsequent Government of

National Defense recognized and feared this composition. So did the Parisian bourgeoisie. As the prominent critic and journalist Francisque Sarcey mused about the city's elite, between the Prussians and "the reds . . . I do not know which of these two ills generated more fear: they had greater hate for the foreigner, they felt greater dread of the *Bellevillois* [residents of the working-class neighborhood of Belleville]."[44] Long-term class tensions permeated this intense moment of dramatic governmental change in the midst of war.

A broad range of factions vied to shape the new republic. Jailed republicans and socialists were freed, some by supporters breaking into prisons to liberate them, such as Henri Rochefort and the Blanquist and future Communard Emile Eudes, others by release under the new republic, including the Internationalists and future Communards Léo Frankel and Benoît Malon. The Empire's collapse also meant that the many socialists and labor activists who had fled France or gone into hiding to escape police harassment and arrest could now return. Many did so immediately. Victor Hugo, the celebrated poet, novelist, intellectual, and politician, returned from nineteen years of self-exile in England. Arriving in Paris, he proclaimed, "Citizens, I have said: the day the Republic returns to France, I will return. I am here."[45]

Varlin arrived from Belgium, where he had taken refuge following his condemnation along with other members of the Paris International earlier that summer. Wasting no time, he and his fellow Internationalists met to reorganize and take action. In the September 6 issue of the newspaper *Le Rappel,* they published an article titled "Organization of Republican Committees in Each Arrondissement," announcing the outcome of a meeting they had held the previous evening, "composed primarily of delegates from workers' societies and from sections of the International." The participants had unanimously agreed to form Republican Committees in all of Paris's twenty arrondissements (the city was—and still is—divided into twenty neighborhood sections, called "arrondissements"), with each sending representatives to form the Central Committee of Twenty Arrondissements. Each arrondissement committee would operate as a vigilance organization, "making themselves available to the provisional government, to execute measures of order, and to actively assist, with the greatest devotion, in the defense of the capital."[46]

Two days earlier, on September 4, the Paris International had issued an appeal "To the German People," calling for a Prussian retreat from French soil and an end to the war. Underscoring the emperor's fall, the Internationalists affirmed, "the man who unleashed this fratricidal conflict . . . no longer exists for us." Instead, they offered, "Republican France invites you, in the name of justice, to withdraw your arms. . . . The French people are the friend and ally of all free people. . . . Through our alliance, let us found the UNITED STATES OF EUROPE."[47] As the name implied, the International sought to unite socialists and working people across borders. Making clear that the emperor had instigated the war, of which they wanted no part, the Paris section urged the Prussian people to make peace. In the meantime, the Parisians took a pragmatic and patriotic stance.

Like the Internationalists, the Blanquists (the more radical revolutionary socialists) also rallied to defend France. The common thread tying together France's political factions—from the Blanquists on the far left, through the Internationalists, to the moderate republicans (the majority of the government), and the right-wing monarchists—was the professed patriotic desire to defend France against the Prussians. Yet the right and many in the center, and the elites they represented, still held profound fear of the socialists and the working people they sought to represent.

The People's Arc

While political factions jostled for power, the people of Paris exulted in the freedom and potential of the new republic. Across the city, they organized to push the nascent government toward democratic, egalitarian goals, fighting its conservative tendencies. Simultaneously, working people rallied to defend the republic against its military opponent, Prussia. In addition to joining Republican

Committees in many of the arrondissements, citizens formed political clubs. At a September 9 meeting of Blanqui's club, La Patrie en Danger ("The Nation in Danger"), *citoyen* Balsenq "asked that the churches be used for the national defense"; *citoyen* Cartier "called for the creation of establishments to care for children whose parents were fighting the enemy"; and *citoyenne* ("woman citizen") Emery "proposed organizing in every arrondissement a field hospital, where women . . . by aiding the wounded, would participate in the defense and triumph of the republic."[48] Clubs provided locations for men and women to express their resentments, fears, and desires. Successors in many ways to the public meetings of the late Empire, they continued as the locales where argument and speech could reshape public opinion. *Citoyen* Balsenq's request reflected both the strong current of anticlericalism among socialists and swaths of the working class, as well as the presence of revolutionary memory—during the French Revolution, the state had nationalized the Catholic Church and its properties. *Citoyen* Cartier's call for childcare indicated the economic and social realities shaping the lives of poor people at war, while reflecting both men's and women's participation in the conflict. *Citoyenne* Emery's proposal typified working-class Parisian women's defense engagements. All these concerns would carry over into the Commune.

The Prussians proved unmoved by the International's pleas for peace. On September 17, Prussian forces laid siege to Paris. They allowed people in and out of the city but blocked goods. Increasing numbers of wealthy people fled. Food prices skyrocketed as provisions became scarce. Journalist Francisque Sarcey lamented the price of a "good chicken," normally 3 francs to 3 francs 50 centimes, "is today 14 to 15 francs . . . dried vegetables, beans, lentils, peas . . . are no longer for sale. Before disappearing, they were sold for four times their former value."[49] Butter prices increased eightfold, potatoes by ten times, and eggs by 1,400 percent. The government rationed meat in October, and later bread; it requisitioned all edible animals, ultimately including horses (the consumption of which increased during the siege).[50] People ate dogs, cats, and rats.

Such deprivation, however, did not affect the upper classes. Restaurants and elite homes paid exorbitant prices for now-rare foodstuffs. A theater of elite "siege cuisine" emerged, as exotic zoo animals, including elephants, zebras, reindeer, and camels, were slaughtered. Under the guise of feeding the hungry, the butchery instead enabled bourgeois diners to perform a kind of patriotic "sacrifice" by eating the animals. Never reaching the poor, the meat instead appeared on menus in the most exclusive restaurants, such as Voisin's Christmas 1870 menu, which included "English-style roasted camel," "side of bear with pepper sauce," and "terrine of antelope with truffles."[51]

For the politically centrist Sarcey, later a virulent anti-Communard, "The class on which the extreme costliness of food weighed heaviest was the petite bourgeoisie [small shopkeepers] . . . those who lived day to day . . . in the space between poverty and ease. . . . They were too proud to expose their need to the public. . . . They endured cruel privations with a resignation that touched on heroism."[52] Rather than identifying the working class as suffering most from enormously inflated food prices, Sarcey sympathized with the shame that small shopkeepers felt in falling into poverty due to the siege. He failed to recognize how, for the working class, the siege increasingly meant hunger nearing starvation. Nathalie Lemel's food cooperative La Marmite served meals to the poor, while also providing needed conviviality and encouraging Internationalist politics, in its four locations. Charles Keller, a well-known singer and member of the International who periodically performed at La Marmite, explained, "While renowned singers appeared before the 'clients' . . . Nathalie Lemel did not sing, she philosophized and resolved major problems simply and with extraordinary ease."[53] Another member of the International and a future Communard, Victorine Brocher, opened a cooperative bakery to help meet food needs.

Socialists and socialist feminists, like Lemel and Brocher, sought communal answers to the challenges of living under siege and at war. In doing so, they created the conditions for workers, women, and the poor to reimagine themselves collectively. Organizations such as the Democratic Society for Moralization by Labor, a mixed group of women and men of which Louise Michel was secretary, supplied fabric to textile workers unemployed as a result of the siege, as well as serving as a clearinghouse for matching workers with employers. Announcing its creation, the Society called for support, stressing that "Poverty and discouragement are great. . . . We have confidence in your patriotism, and we count on you."[54] Seeking to ameliorate the economic hardship brought by war and siege, the organization appealed to both a communal and a national sense of solidarity and support.

With similar goals, an announcement "To the Women of Paris," signed by the highly engaged Michel and twelve other women, urged, "It is up to us to give moral support to the men who defend . . . the soil of our dear country."[55] Encouraging women to encourage their spouses in arms, the appeal went further, counseling women to push their husbands into radical republicanism. Asking "Do they have no opinion?" it suggests "We must make them [republicans] despite themselves." Pressing beyond women's traditional affirming spousal role, the appeal called on women to advance the republican cause not only in sustaining the soldiers defending the cause, but also by aggressively promoting republicanism.

In this moment of governmental and societal flux, women's wartime roles—like women's status more broadly—expanded even in the face of scrutiny and contestation. André Léo, in a letter to the newspaper *La Petite Presse*, declared, "Women are no less courageous than men . . . they are indispensable to the defense." She argued that women could fulfill "nearly all public services" including "the post office . . . typography, making cartridges and equipment." Promoting war production and home-front work for women, Léo reimagined women's labor. Yet these were couched in distinct gender roles: "to the women the care of life, to the men that of death. But all in the service of the nation."[56] Addressing both women's desire for patriotic participation and Paris's need for workers to conduct production and public services, Léo urged an expansion of women's acceptable labor and sphere. This not only helped meet wartime needs, but also advanced feminist goals. The new and fragile republic required support, while also providing an opportunity to increase women's rights and freedoms. Like the call "To the Women of Paris" during the Prussian siege, Léo asserted a moderate, yet nonrevolutionary, alteration in women's roles. The overwhelming majority of socialists and working-class Parisians supported France continuing the war with Prussia, despite the profound hardship it brought. Widespread suspicion of the Government of National Defense's commitment to the fight intensified as news reached Paris of troop retreats, secret negotiations with the enemy, and finally General Bazaine's surrender of more than 60,000 soldiers. Bazaine's capitulation convinced many Parisians that the provisional Government of National Defense and its military would soon overthrow the republican government. On October 31, protesters from the working-class quarters flooded the city center, incited by socialist newspapers, political clubs, republican vigilance committees, and a general public outcry. Among the sea of people and placards filling the plaza in front of the Hôtel de Ville (City Hall), an enormous sign read "Long Live the Republic! No Armistice! The Commune! Death to the Cowards!"[57] Blanquists, National Guardsmen, and other militants invaded the Hôtel de Ville and declared an end to the Government of National Defense.

They did not succeed: immediate infighting and a lack of coordination prevented the would-be insurgents from taking control of the government. But the political temperature of the city rose after this failed uprising. Parisians formed more political clubs and vigilance committees.[58] Calls for a "revolutionary Commune"—first heard a year earlier in the public meetings—spread.[59] Hunger, deprivation, and discontent increased. In the depth of winter, during months of only eight hours of daylight, oil and coal ran out, plunging Paris into darkness and cold as the year ended, the siege continued, and 1871 began.

Yet another battlefield defeat—one with over four thousand casualties—led to a subsequent near-insurrection on January 22, during which shots from the Hôtel de Ville killed five protesters. That evening, the government announced the closing of all political clubs, accusing them of "criminal excitation" and "civil war." As

Louise Michel reproached, "the name 'Republic'" had become "only a mask"; in the name of order, the government betrayed the goal of popular participation.[60]

The following week, France surrendered to Prussia. In a treaty seen by many as a profound capitulation, France agreed to pay an indemnity to the victors and to surrender the French territories of Alsace and Lorraine. This triumph allowed Prussia's leader Otto von Bismarck to unify and create the German Empire. Highlighting France's disgrace in defeat, Bismarck declared the new German Empire in the Great Hall of Mirrors in France's Versailles Palace. Paule Mink described Parisians "shuddering with sadness and rage" at the capitulation.[61]

The January 28 armistice required ratification by a representative Assembly within three weeks. The Government of National Defense resigned, and elections for a new National Assembly were set for February 8. With only eleven days to prepare, and in this moment of crisis, France elected a conservative, monarchist-dominated government. Adolphe Thiers became head of state. Thus, this antirepublican government was charged with sustaining the five-month-old republic under German occupation, with a capital populated by a war-battered, highly politicized population that seethed with anger and frustration at the betrayal it felt at its government's ignominious surrender.

The military was ill-prepared to confront popular discontent. The armistice had allowed food into the desperate capital. It also mandated the disarming of a quarter of a million French soldiers in Paris. The truce excepted only 12,000 National Guardsmen, those charged with maintaining order in the city. Minimally trained and inconsistently armed, the National Guard drew from both working-class and elite communities. But after the armistice, guardsmen from the upper classes increasingly forsook the ranks. A newly formed Central Committee of the National Guard emerged as a radicalized political force. The Parisian International initially resisted allying with the Guard because of the International's opposition to nationalist goals. Varlin ultimately convinced the organization, arguing pragmatically and successfully that "if we remain isolated in the face of such a force, our influence will disappear. But if we unite with this Committee, we will take a great step toward a socialist future."[62] He would subsequently be elected to the Central Committee of the National Guard from Paris's seventeenth arrondissement.

In early March, the monarchist-dominated National Assembly enacted a series of economic and political measures intended to restore "order" and suppress opposition in the turbulent city. The Assembly terminated the National Guard's daily pay, the only income for many of its members, seeking to weaken this armed, potentially insurgent force. Rents and the payment of small business credits had been suspended during the siege; the new government made all rents and debts immediately payable, with interest, virtually overnight. Mass evictions soon followed, as did economic catastrophes for some middle-class Parisians. In a further attack on the working class, the Assembly lifted the moratorium on the sale of goods deposited at the Mont de Piété, the national pawnshop. In the deep economic hardship brought by war and siege, desperate people had pawned cooking pots, mattresses, workers' tools, or anything of any value. Most lacked the ability to immediately reclaim these vital goods. Allowing their sale to others put them permanently out of reach. In a direct political strike at the opposition, the government shut down much of the socialist press. Finally, the government abandoned Paris and established itself in Versailles, the semirural traditional seat of royal power. Many saw this as an affront to the people of Paris and the capital of the republic and revolutions. Yet another wave of wealthy Parisians fled the city, following their government to an enclave of opulence and plenty, in stark contrast to the unsettled, dispossessed, radicalized place they left behind.

In Paris, the working class feared both the new government and the Prussian army (which remained on French soil), but still supported the National Guard, identifying with its grassroots formation and recognizing it as the people's army. Despite unemployment and dire want, during the siege Parisian workers had contributed to arming the Guard with cannons. Michel explained this perspective: "these National Guard cannons were purchased by subscription, and belonged to them for the defense of Paris."[63] Before the Prussians had entered the city in late February, during what Léo termed "a night of indignation and tumult, justly defiant crowds" claimed the artillery from the bourgeois neighborhoods.[64] Michel described how "men, women, and children hitched up cannons" and dragged them across the city to their own neighborhoods, including to the heights of "Montmartre, rolling them up the Boulevard Ornano, mounting them on the Butte."[65]

Thiers would not allow the cannons to remain in the working-class quarters, particularly on the butte of Montmartre, where, as Léo described, the artillery was "turned toward the center of the city, toward the city of luxury and palaces, of monarchical plots, of infamous speculators, and of cowardly governments."[66] On March 17, the Versailles government posted announcements on walls across Paris, proclaiming, "In your interest, and that of your city, the government is resolved to act. . . . The cannons stolen from the State will be restored to the arsenals . . . the government counts on your cooperation. . . . The good citizens must separate themselves from the bad . . . restoring order is necessary at any price, even the use of force."[67] In the 4:00 A.M. darkness on March 18, the government took action. Installing thousands of troops at strategic locations across the capital, Thiers sent battalions to Montmartre, ascending the butte from two directions. Versailles officer Eugène Hennebert later recounted that by sunrise "the support troops controlled all of the important points. All that remained was to take the artillery, and the success would be complete."[68] But the teams of horses needed to pull the cannons failed to arrive.

During what Hennebert called "this fatal delay," Montmartre began to awaken. Michel, among the first to encounter the troops, ran down the butte, rifle under her coat, shouting for reinforcements. On her return, she later recalled, "we climbed the Butte, knowing that a battle-ready army waited at the summit." Expecting a slaughter, instead she found "the Butte enveloped in a white light, a splendid dawn of deliverance. . . . It was not death that awaited us on the Buttes . . . but the surprise of the people's victory."[69] While the soldiers awaited the teams of horses, church bells sounded the alarm, and the people of Montmartre streamed from their houses. National Guardsman Sutter-Laumann exulted, "the women threw themselves in front of the troops' guns, and the troops reversed. . . . It was intoxicating, a triumph!"[70] Most of the soldiers were young, working-class Parisian men, now surrounded by a growing sea of women who offered them food and wine and reminded them they, too, belonged to the people. Soldiers fraternized with protesters. Lifting their rifle butts in the air, refusing orders to fire on the crowd, they turned and arrested their leaders.

By the time the horses finally arrived, a small military remnant tried to move the cannons themselves. According to an anonymous author, Montmartre women shouted, "Unharness the horses! . . . We want the cannons! We will have the cannons!" and National Guardsmen cut the leads that attached the horses to the artillery.[71] The Central Committee of the National Guard sent word to neighborhood battalions. Varlin led 1,500 Guards from the working-class quarters of Montmartre and Batignolles into elite parts of the city, as other battalions spread out to occupy government sites including police headquarters and ultimately the Hôtel de Ville.[72] Before the end of the day, General Claude Lecomte, who had ordered the troops to shoot at the defenders of the cannon, and General Clement Thomas, long hated for his role in the brutal repression of the 1848 Revolution, lay dead, shot by the Montmartre crowd. A London *Times* journalist witnessed as troop fraternization spread. As an army line regiment approached, "the National Guard . . . shouted *'Vive la Republique!'* This seemed to be the signal for the whole of the regular troops to throw the butts of their rifles in the air." He continued: "The soldiers in the balconies and windows, where, I suppose, they had been placed to shoot Guards, came down and embraced them instead; women shed tears of joy, and talked about the sons and brothers who were . . . in the army; arms were intertwined, hands wrung, cheeks kissed." As Louise Michel declared, "the revolution was made."[73] Suddenly, improbably, Parisians controlled Paris.

2

Fluorescence

In the late afternoon of March 18, as soldiers embraced Parisian workers and turned against their military leaders, Adolphe Thiers abandoned Paris for Versailles and ordered the army and government to evacuate the city. In the wake of the humiliation that had occurred that morning in Montmartre, Thiers took drastic measures. To subdue the city he perceived as being in open revolt, Thiers decided to confront it from outside, and with a different kind of troops. Commanding a complete and immediate withdrawal shocked not only conservative politicians and administrators, but also the Central Committee of the Parisian National Guard. The uprising against the Versailles army's efforts to seize the Montmartre cannons that morning had thrust the Central Committee into a position of insurgent leadership. Hours later, Thiers's desertion of the city catapulted the Committee into the role of governing Paris. Victorine Brocher, disbelieving when she heard neighborhood newspaper vendors shouting, "Surprise, Montmartre attacked, cannons taken, National Guard and army fraternize!" headed to the Hôtel de Ville with her husband. "On arrival . . . we saw that the newspaper vendors had spoken the truth. The entire Central Committee was meeting at the Hôtel de Ville. Everyone was so happy, the sun shone, it was a splendid day. Paris, which had sought its own enfranchisement, seemed to breathe healthier air." In the newly liberated city, Brocher enthused, "everyone celebrated . . .

the spectacle of a magnificent military parade, of the *gendarmes* [military police] leaving for Versailles."[1] The "surprise" ricocheted through Paris, and soon, around the world.

As the Versailles troops made their sudden and disordered departure from the city, the Central Committee members debated how best to handle their new and unexpected authority. The capital's multiple political factions deliberated their next steps, while in the streets working-class Parisians celebrated the emancipation of their city.

Emile Duval, head of the National Guard of the thirteenth arrondissement, a working-class area in the southeast of the city, had that afternoon led his regiment northwest to the Préfecture de Police. Headquarters of the city's police force, it was located in the center of the Ile de la Cité, across from the Hôtel de Ville at Paris's geographic and administrative center. That night Duval sent a brief message home: "My dear wife, do not worry about my long absence. I am at the Préfecture de Police, which we captured at midnight with no violence."[2]

By the next morning, the National Guard had occupied all major government buildings, vacated by officials on Thiers's orders. Contrary to Victorine Brocher's understanding that "The entire Central Committee was meeting at the Hôtel de Ville" on March 18, only National Guard representatives from the working-class arrondissements met that day. The conservative, elite parts of the city remained loyal to Thiers. Power appeared to have fallen to the Central Committee of the National Guard, yet the mayors of the city's twenty arrondissements officially held legal administrative control over Paris, authority granted by Thiers when he quit the city. Yet, did legal control matter at this incendiary moment?

The Paris Commune, the luminescent and incendiary event linking revolutionary histories and futures, developed as more than one revolution. The Commune upended political, economic, and sociocultural structures. From the explosive formation of radical government to the establishment of grassroots political clubs, the political revolution involved socialism and anarchism, feminisms, anticlericalism, and the legacies of the French Revolution and

France's Revolution of 1848. The economic revolt centered on the class- and gender-based reorganization and revaluing of labor, the undermining of capitalism, and the centering of cooperation and association. The sociocultural revolution involved the social change that the economic and political revolutions would bring to people's lives. This included legal changes that ended the exclusionary category of "illegitimate" for natural children, recognized free unions as equal to state- and Church-sanctioned marriages, and introduced mandatory secular schooling for girls and boys. Popular festivals, an expansive free press, and an Artists Association were counted among creative sociocultural innovations that altered the texture of life and the parameters of class and gender. The Communards began re-creating the society around them, revolutionizing what a city and a nation could be, expanding opportunities and opening paths to new worlds.

Politics

March 19, a beautiful, sunny Sunday, sparkled with excitement, anticipation, and a significant degree of trepidation. Parisians awoke to the glowing reality that the reactionary government—the one that had introduced punitive measures against the poor and small shop owners, and that many feared was planning to overthrow the republic and reinstate the monarchy—was gone. The city so long dominated by the national government had broken free. A bright air of festivity and triumph filled the streets. Yet those newly propelled to power bore an immense weight, holding in their hands the fate of the City of Light and its citizens. Hoping to reassure those citizens, the Central Committee posted an announcement on walls across the city, "To the People": "The People of Paris have thrown off the yoke imposed on them. Calm, impassive in their power, they waited without fear and without provocation for the shameless fools who wanted to attack the republic. . . . The People of Paris are called . . . to hold communal elections."[3] The Central Committee of the National Guard signaled their intent to relinquish power to a political body representative of the people.

Questions of legitimacy and legality immediately emerged as highly contested flash points in the negotiations over power and control of Paris. At the Central Committee's March 19 meeting, the Blanquists, including Duval (who had seized the Prefecture of Police) and Théophile Ferré, argued for immediate military action against Versailles, seeking to take advantage of the army's present state of disarray. The moderate socialists on the Committee, including Varlin, resisted. Contending that their role consisted of protecting municipal rights, the fight for which had underlain the uprising, this faction insisted on electing a government that would then have legitimacy. The Central Committee clarified this position in a second proclamation, one directed to the National Guard on March 19: "You have charged us with organizing the defense of Paris and of your rights. We know we have accomplished this mission, aided by your generous courage and your admirable calm. We have chased out this treasonous government. Now, our mandate is expired. . . . Prepare to hold communal elections and give yourselves the one thing that we could barely hope for, the establishment of the true republic."[4] The Central Committee's statements and actions reflected the dominance of the Internationalists, the moderate, associationist socialists, in the group; they strove for the organization and empowerment of the working class. In contrast, the Blanquists sought the overthrow of the bourgeois order by a small, conspiratorial group of revolutionaries. Louise Michel, a Blanquist at this point (her politics would change dramatically after the Commune), lamented the Committee's refusal to attack Versailles militarily: "If these devoted men had had less respect for legality, it would have been aptly named the Revolutionary Commune on the road to Versailles."[5] She also regretted not taking more dramatic action, affirming "I would have, without blanching . . . taken the life" of Thiers. "Rivers of blood would not have flowed, piles of dead as high as mountains would not have filled Paris and turned it into a mass grave." She believed that if she "had killed Thiers in the Assembly," in the midst of the Versailles government, "the resultant terror would have stopped the reaction. . . . Our two lives would have prevented the slaughter of Paris." To Michel, adhering to law at the hour of insurgency contradicted and undercut the revolutionary circumstances.

One of the most renowned Communards, Michel was born in 1830 in the village of Vroncourt, and was raised by her mother, an unmarried domestic servant, and her provincial bourgeois paternal grandparents, who acknowledged and supported Louise as their grandchild. Trained as a teacher, Michel moved to Paris in 1856 and became increasingly politically involved. Interested not just in educational practice but also theory, she was drawn to feminism and socialism as ways of addressing the inequities she observed around her. When Michel cofounded La Société du droit des femmes, "The Society for Women's Rights," with André Léo and Paule Mink in 1866, she supported rights-based feminism. Increasingly involved in the International, she soon moved to a feminist version of the more radical revolutionary Blanquism. Michel subsequently abandoned the idea that changes in women's legal rights could remedy gender-based oppressions. "The issue of political rights is dead," she declared.[6] Turning to revolutionary socialist feminism, she sought the overthrow of the existing order in favor of one more radically egalitarian. The experience of the Commune and its repression would lead her to another ideological shift in its aftermath. Identifying the failures of top-down Blanquist revolutionary socialism, she came to embrace anarchism and with it decentralized power. Yet at the beginning of the insurgency, she allied closely with the Blanquist faction.

Blanquists made up the majority of key administrative officers appointed by the Central Committee on March 19,[7] including Duval and Raoul Rigault to head the Ex-Prefecture of Police, Emile Eudes to lead the Ministry of War, and François Jourde and Varlin to direct finances. All except Varlin were Blanquists. The Committee also voted amnesty to all political prisoners, and ended military courts' rule over Parisian civil matters, thus immediately restoring democratic judicial procedures. At the same time, Thiers issued a statement intended to inflame passions against the insurrectionists. "The government, elected by universal suffrage, has declared several times that it wants to found the republic. Those who want to overthrow it are the men of disorder, the assassins who do not fear horror and death in a city that can only save itself with calm and the respect of laws. . . . The crimes of these men will, we hope, incite the just indignation of the Paris population, who will stand up to inflict on them the punishment they merit."[7] Thiers heightened the stakes. Laying blame for the crowd's spontaneous murder of the two generals squarely at the feet of the uprising's leaders, Thiers employed the classic language of order versus disorder. Elsewhere, he accused the Central Committee of being a "shadow" group of unknown men acting under cover—despite their signatures appearing on every proclamation. Invoking a dark, brutal, and threatening image of the revolutionaries' vision, Thiers incited Parisians to rise up against them. The monarchist head of a monarchist-dominated National Assembly claimed the role of protector of the republic. The next night Duval, on his third night holding the Prefecture of Police, sent another note to his wife, "My dear wife, Be kind enough to bring me some clothes and my revolver."[8]

Although Thiers claimed his government was elected by "universal suffrage," women remained disenfranchised under France's Napoleonic Civil Code of Law. While feminists had focused on gaining political rights under the Empire, the Commune brought larger possibilities. They saw the potential of liberation expand beyond parity with men under an oppressive regime. Working-class women sought concrete change in their lives, not merely the ability to vote. Suffrage had an abstract value, one recognized primarily by those without day-to-day survival concerns. Most bourgeois feminists, along with the majority of the city's elites, had fled Paris under the Prussian siege, and more left after March 18. The feminists who remained in Paris, primarily socialists and members of the working class, sought change not only regarding gender, but also class—for both personal and political reasons.

Between March 19 and March 26, Paris hung suspended between revolution and conciliation. The Central Committee sought the support of the city's officially appointed arrondissement mayors, as Committee member Edouard Moreau stated, "to make the situation regular," in the hopes of gaining legitimization and popular support for their upcoming elections.[9] Days of discussion and debate illuminated the lack of agreement not just between the two bodies, but also within each. The most conservative mayors supported Versailles; some republican mayors feared the monarchist-dominated National Assembly would try to reinstate an Orleanist prince; others hoped for a negotiated end to the conflict; and none fully supported the Central Committee. In the meantime, street conflicts arose between supporters of Versailles and those of the National Guard Committee. Across France, cities emulated Paris as insurgents rose up and took power in Narbonne, Lyon, Marseille, Saint-Étienne, and the industrial city La Creusot—the politicized site of bloody strikes the previous year. As the *Chicago Tribune* alerted its readers, "The Revolution Is Spreading." While the provincial uprisings reflected the extent of boiling-point social pressures in France, the Chicago newspaper's alarm indicated the international fear inspired by Paris's insurgency. The *Tribune* report continued breathlessly, "The Hôtel de Ville is surmounted by the red flag . . . respectable Parisians are stupefied. . . . The wine shops are open; drunkenness is rampant. Even the women are armed."[10] Their inversion of class hierarchy (the red flag of revolution marking leftist control of City Hall, stupefying "respectable" Parisians) and gender norms (women with guns) were seen as an emergent global menace. The world awaited Thiers and the National Assembly's next step.

After hostile, high-stakes negotiations, the Assembly refused to recognize the Parisian elections. This indicated the national government's broader repudiation of the legitimacy of the municipal independence of Paris. During this week, Thiers had brought troops to Versailles from across France. Distrusting the loyalty of Paris-based soldiers, Thiers amassed an army of provincial men, relying on their enmity toward the capital. On March 25, the arrondissement mayors (with the exception of the two most conservative) finally issued a statement supporting the vote, "[c]onvinced that [they were] the only way to avoid civil war and a Parisian bloodletting, while also affirming the republic."[11] Thiers responded that

2.1. "For those who have, things are going badly!! For those who have not, things are going well!!" Post card. Wikimedia Commons.

the elections would be "without liberty or moral authority." Instead, he declared, "Order will be established in Paris."[12]

The March 26 elections enacted a further break with Versailles, as the newly chosen Commune Council claimed municipal sovereignty in clear opposition to the nation. With 40 percent overall voter turnout (and much higher in working-class districts), the left won the day. Paris chose a young administration, with an average age of thirty-seven. As Élie Reclus, the future head of France's National Library under the Commune, extolled, "All of the winners are . . . enemies of bourgeoisism and friends of the proletariat; all are . . . red [radical] adversaries of blue [moderate] republicans. On this memorable day, the Social Revolution won the election."[13] The new government concretized class alliances and divisions, fueling Versailles's fear and hatred, and electrifying the people of Paris.

The Commune government consisted of three political groups. The socialist Internationalists included Varlin and Vallès. The Blanquists, including Duval and Ferré, were small in number but increasingly influential. The third faction, the Jacobins, consisted predominantly of older men, including veterans of the Revolution of 1848 such as journalists Charles Delescluze and Felix Pyat. Harkening back to their forebears who had taken over the French Revolution in 1793, they argued for centralizing authority in the government. But the tenuous nature of the Commune, along with the activists on the streets, undermined their project.

Two days after the election, a ceremony at the Hôtel de Ville inaugurated the new Commune Council. Louise Michel described the "splendid" event where a "human sea" gathered, and cries of "Vive la Commune!" filled the air. The sun shone on the crowds in front of the red-swathed Hôtel de Ville. The newspaper *Le Cri du peuple,* edited by newly elected Commune Council member Jules Vallès, exulted, "The Commune is proclaimed. It has come from the ballot box, triumphant, sovereign, and armed. The Commune is proclaimed on a day of revolutionary and patriotic festivities, peaceful and joyous."[14] Using sexualized and familial language to gender the Commune and citizens as male, the article rejoiced in the "citizen-soldier" fertilizing the newly revolutionized city. "Today idea weds revolution. Tomorrow the citizen-soldier, in order to fertilize the just-married and acclaimed municipality, must retake his place at the workbench, always proud but now free. After the poetry of triumph, the prose of work." The statement reflects assumptions of citizenship as male, and about the political centrality of men's labor. It also underscored the importance of "the ballot box" to the Commune being "triumphant, sovereign, and armed," emphasizing the revolutionaries' focus on legality.

The Commune envisioned itself as embodying all Parisian citizens. On the day of its inauguration, the government issued its first official statement, assuring Parisians, "You are the masters of your destiny; with your support, the representation that you have established will repair the disasters created by the disgraced power."[15] They spoke of themselves as chosen by the newly liberated people to rectify, with the support of the people, the calamitous situation created by Thiers and his government. Rather than a representative system, the Communards conceptualized their government as a direct democracy, one in which all elected positions were revocable. They believed that the source of all power rested with the people.[16]

The voters, however, included only half of the adult population. Elected through universal male suffrage, the Commune Council was chosen by only the male portion of the population. Women remained disenfranchised from electoral politics, both literally and in its imagery, as exemplified by the *Le Cri du peuple* statement. Yet most women sought neither the vote nor a formal governing role. Socialist feminists considered the Commune the dawn of the social revolution and saw new political forms on the horizon. They understood the Commune as transitional to an emergent, egalitarian society. Female Communards engaged extensively, however, in a broad range of political acts, actions that constituted politics outside of government.

Working-class women and men enthusiastically and avidly participated in political clubs. An outgrowth of the public meetings of the late Empire, and of the political clubs banned during the Prussian siege, political clubs re-emerged with the Commune. These organizations evolved as arenas of popular sovereignty, as locations for grassroots political expression and engagement. Working-class *clubistes*, as the participants were known, developed political positions in arguments and speeches. Their stances resulted from their lived experiences of class-based exploitation and marginalization, their conscious perpetuation of France's revolutionary tradition, and their deep anticlericalism. *Clubistes* advocated cooperation and association, ideas antithetical to capitalism and fundamental to labor and many socialist movements. A significant number of Commune government members took part in the clubs, including Théophile Ferré and Henri Rochefort, and some well-known *communardes* (the word for female *communards*), including

Louise Michel and Paule Mink, spoke in political clubs.[17] The meetings, nonetheless, remained spaces of organic working-class exposition and engagement, examples of lively and extensive politics beyond government. For *clubiste* women, subjugation in the family and their particularly gendered experiences in the workplace—doubly exploited as both laborers and women—contributed to their radicalization. All of these issues came to the fore in the clubs.

Although the Commune government was a revolutionary regime, the people in the political clubs tended to take even more radical positions. Whereas the Commune Council strove for legalism and legitimacy, most *clubistes* did not.

Nealy all political clubs met in churches. Reviving a tradition of the French Revolution, Communards appropriated these spaces of power, wealth, and authority. Frequently the largest and most imposing structures in their neighborhoods, churches loomed physically, and because France had no separation between church and state (something the Commune would change), the Catholic Church, the official church, had dominated politically. The Church controlled education, supported conservative politics, displayed enormous riches, and its clergy and dogma permeated intimate family and community relationships. Political clubs convened in approximately 50 percent of Paris's fifty-one churches, a significant spatial and ideological claim. In these contexts, working-class and socialist Parisians vehemently articulated hostilities and resentments. As Benoît Malon, Commune member and romantic partner of André Léo, explained, "This pulpit, where Catholic priests had recently preached respect for power and resignation to poverty, was now wrapped in red banners. . . . From there improvised orators preach, in the light of profane candles, the holy revolt of the poor, the exploited, the oppressed, against the tyrants, exciting passions for the decisive battle from which the political and social enfranchisement of the people will arise."[18] The clubs inverted major hierarchies—of religion, class, and, when women spoke, gender—jolting the status quo in multiple ways.

Women and men joined many mixed-sex clubs, but male-only and female-only political clubs also operated across the city.

Communard and journalist Prosper-Olivier Lissagaray wrote about one women's organization: "They have a special club in the Batignolles where they discuss war and peace. Even if few precise ideas come from these feverish meetings, they provide combustion and courage for many."[19] Lissagaray thus lauded the revolutionary enthusiasm while also denigrating the participants' intellects and rationality. In these arenas, activist women discussed not only the issues engaged in male clubs, but also the particularly gendered realities of women's lives: the ways in which they experienced politics, work, family, and religion.

Many women used clubs to assert their dissatisfaction with male authority. At a club on the Boulevard d'Italie, a female speaker asserted men's weakness and underscored their political failures. Suggesting women's readiness to expand their roles, she argued "Men . . . are like monarchs softened by possessing too much authority. . . . It is time for woman to replace man in directing public affairs."[20] Marie Catherine Rogissart, a dressmaker and the vice president of Club Saint-Éloi, also alleged male inaction. At a May club meeting, Rogissart demanded, "You must fight against the Versaillaises assassins, or we will tear out your livers!"[21] Using dramatic language to express frustration with the existing military situation, Rogissart subsequently became involved in a women's battalion in the twelfth arrondissement and worked actively to search for National Guard deserters. The club provided her a public forum to discuss, and possibly to organize to remedy, her political concerns.

The author Marforio, pseudonym of Louise Lacroix, reported that the orator at the Club d'Italie, the woman who described men as like "soft monarchs," was a teacher who "spoke a more correct French than the habitual language of *citoyennes* . . . at these sorts of meetings."[22] While educated women did participate in certain clubs, like high-profile *communardes* Michel and Mink, working-class women made up the majority. Clubs provided them a forum for expressing anger at the systems of oppression that had long subjugated them, including the government, bosses, husbands, and the Catholic Church.

Clubistes expressed strong and often verbally violent anticlericalism, frequently directing their hostility toward the representatives of the Church. According to the anti-Communard observer Paul Fontoulieu, during an April 16 meeting in l'Eglise Saint-Eloi, *citoyenne* Morel suggested they "throw all nuns into the River Seine," accusing those serving as nurses of poisoning hospitalized Communard soldiers.[23] At St. Elisabeth du Temple, Fontoulieu recounted, *citoyenne* Lablanc declared, "We must flay the priests alive, and build barricades with their bodies."[24] The rhetorical violence reflected the intensity of working-class resentment toward the Church. What these women said and where they said it—anticlerical orations, spoken in churches—intensified *communardes'* perceived threat to orders of gender and religious authority.

Hostile to all *clubistes,* the anti-Communard Fontoulieu held particular contempt for the women. He considered the idea of female orators to be unnatural, describing women as "horrible . . . savage priestesses of Death."[25] Women speaking publicly challenged the era's dominant gender roles. Their status as working class added further affront. Fontoulieu described *citoyenne* Thourout, a battlefield cook who spoke at the Club Saint-Sèverin, as "fiery, hotheaded, and drunk on communalism."[26] Neither "fiery" nor "hotheaded" fell within bourgeois categories of acceptable female behavior, nor did drunkenness. Identifying one of the central tenets of the Commune, communalism, as an intoxicant, Fontoulieu assumed that a politicized woman—a supporter of communalism—could not possibly have rationally chosen those politics. Instead, she was "drunk" on them.

Because of the grassroots nature of the clubs, most documentation comes from observers like Lissagaray, Malon, or the anti-Communard Paul Fontoulieu. Yet some political clubs did leave first-person records. The Club des Prolétaires published four issues of a newspaper, *Le Prolétaire,* in the Commune's final weeks. The Club Saint-Sèverin adopted a slate of propositions on how to revive Paris's economy, and the newspaper *Paris-Libre* subsequently printed them. In a different format, the Club Saint-Nicolas des Champs published a community bulletin, a one-sheet flyer, urging "People, govern yourselves—through your public meetings, your press, pressure those who represent you; they will never be revolutionary enough."[27] Many club meetings directed questions and suggestions to the Commune, and they expected answers. In these ways, clubs exercised popular sovereignty, influencing the Commune government from the grass roots.

Some *clubistes* went further in their anticlericalism, rejecting the idea of religion and God. As an orator at Saint-Sulpice cried out, "God . . . you do not exist. You are an invention of the priests. If you exist, then I provoke and defy you. If you are not a coward, you will descend on this altar that we have profaned, and I will plunge my knife in your heart!"[28] This denial of God broke with the French Revolutionary tradition of attacking the institution of the Church, rather than the overall concepts of belief and deity. Other Communards did, however, remain loyal to the Church, and most churches used as political clubs remained open to the faithful during the day, while clubs met in the evenings. But anticlericalism undergirded most politics during the Commune, as it had in the Great Revolution.

While both the Commune leadership and the *clubistes* condemned the authority and wealth of the Catholic Church, the leadership did not express it with such rhetorical brutality. Instead, on April 2, the Commune Council voted for the separation of Church and state, terminating funding for all ecclesiastical institutions, and declaring the secularization of all education. Twenty days later they mandated all religious persons and images be removed from hospitals and prisons. They sought an institutional sweeping away of the influence and power of the Catholic Church.

Revolutionary governing involved enormous challenges and complications. The Commune Council bore the daunting burdens of not only executing municipal governance and administration, but also, as a new and revolutionary body, of creating its form and function as it went along. Blanquists dominated and, allied with the Jacobins, become known as "the majority," while the antiauthoritarian, associationist socialists (mostly Internationalists), made up "the minority." Concurrently, the Central Committee of the National Guard, which had surrendered power to the elected Commune Council, immediately reconstituted itself as a "guardian of the revolution." Having ensured the legitimacy of the governing body through elections, it stood vigilant in protecting the workers' interests. Along with pressures from political clubs and arrondissement committees, this "dynamic between powers that reciprocally limit each other," as political theorist Massimiliano Tomba terms it, existed as an alternative form of politics that rejected the opposition between the governed and the governing.[29] Within this experimental framework, the Central Committee and the Commune Council emerged as parallel and often conflicting powers.[30] Discord also increased between the factions within the Council as the multifaceted pressures escalated.

Simultaneously, the Commune authorities shouldered the reality of fighting a civil war. Despite Paris's extensive efforts to negotiate, Thiers and the National Assembly refused to recognize the Communards as legitimate political opponents, categorizing them instead as criminals and rioters. Thiers seized the opportunity to carry out his threats to restore order to Paris by any means. While Communards and moderate Republicans attempted negotiation, Thiers built an army of 130,000 well-armed, well-rationed, and well-trained soldiers.[31] He had pledged to crush "the vile multitude." As historian John Merriman asserts, "The conservative National Assembly revolted against Paris, and not the other way around."[32]

In the meantime, the Commune government took immediate first steps to better the lives of Parisians. They enacted political measures with significant economic and social impact. At the Commune Council's second meeting, on March 29, it prohibited both evictions for nonpayment of rent and the sale of goods held at the national pawnshop, the Mont de Piété. The Commune thus reversed two harsh measures the Government of National Defense had recently taken against working- and middle-class Parisians. The revolutionary government also assured provisions for the city, attentive to the extreme shortages and hardship caused by the Prussian siege. Barring the export of any food product and opening subsidized municipal butcher shops and markets in every arrondisse-ment, the Commune successfully avoided food scarcity, even after the Versailles army laid siege to Paris.

The Commune Council also expanded the recipients of National Guard widows' pensions to include women in free unions, *unions libres*, with fallen guardsmen. A substantial portion of the work-ing class had entered into *unions libres* rather than legal marriage. They rejected state- and church-sanctioned matrimony because of both their refutation of church authority and their resistance to pay-ing the priests for the marriage ceremony. As André Léo explained, "most of these households have the same regularity as legal mar-riages; they raise their children, have the same sense of commu-nity, and call themselves wife, husband, father, and mother."[33] Yet women in *unions libres* faced moral condemnation from bourgeois authorities. By placing free unions on a par with legal marriage, the Commune circumvented the state and church's authority to sanc-tion marital relationships, while acknowledging the social and eco-nomic reality of many working-class families. Recognizing *union libres* also effectively ended the category of "illegitimacy" and the stigma associated with it.

Outside the city, fighting intensified through April, while inside the Commune government, tensions mounted between the major-ity and minority. On May 1, the Commune Council voted to cre-ate a Committee of Public Safety, an extrajudicial body made up of five members of the Commune Council, answerable to it alone. An emergency measure taken in the face of military crisis, the Committee of Public Safety resurrected the name of a similar body created by the Jacobins during the French Revolution, confronting internal counterrevolution and external invasion. The Committee evoked the authoritarian measures of the 1790s Revolutionary Ter-ror and countered the Commune government's ongoing efforts at associationism and socialist democracy. At the same time, nongov-ernmental organizations and movements across the city continued to initiate new plans for cooperative economic and sociocultural programs, bringing egalitarian ideals to life. While harkening back to multiple French Revolutionary traditions, Communards also innovated and looked forward. As journalist Felix Pyat wrote, "Citizens, you have made a revolution without historical precedent."

Economics

At the May 12 meeting of the Club Saint-Éloi, a speaker named Philippe pronounced, "We are going to found a new society, a truly democratic and social society, where there will never be rich or poor, where if there are rich . . . they will be obligated to surrender their property to the poor."[34] Fontoulieu reported that the crowd responded with "prolonged bravos, frenetic applause," and someone shouted, "Let's start by making Rothschild cough up!" referring to the wealthy banker and regent of the Bank of France.[35] Class-based resentments undergirded the civil war. From the opposite perspective, on March 28 conservative writer and observer Edmond de Goncourt lamented, "Very simply, what is happening is the conquest of France by the workers. . . . The government is passing from the hands of those who have, to those who have not, from those who have a material interest in the conservation of society, to those completely disinterested in order, stability, or conservation. The workers are convulsive agents of destruction and dissolution."[36] A significant portion of the Commune's political conflicts emerged from such long-term, intense socioeconomic antagonisms. The gulf between the poor and the rich involved more than money; it was gendered and interlaced with politics and culture. On the working-class side, the range of socialisms and socialist feminisms that flowered during the Commune reflected the multiple approaches and goals of the era's leftist politics. The inequities of capital and labor formed the economic core of their concerns. On the elite side, the bourgeoisie and aristocracy, through conservative republican and monarchist parties, fought to maintain dominance over wealth and its creation. Versailles's ferocious reaction to Communard efforts illuminates the elites' profound investment in the status quo, and their deep fear and hatred of those upending it.

Like all governments, the Commune needed money to function. Varlin and François Jourde, delegates to the Finance Committee of the National Guard, and subsequently to the Commune government's Finance Commission, immediately focused on paying National Guard members the daily stipend on which many of them and their families survived. On March 19, the two men approached the Bank of France for a line of credit in the name of municipal Paris. Varlin had proposed taking over the national bank, as the Commune took over other institutions including the Prefecture of Police, the Post Office, and the National Library, but the Central Committee and then the Commune Council rejected the move in favor of a legalistic revolutionary path. The bank granted Varlin and Jourde's request, and the National Guards received their pay that same night.[37] Four days later, Varlin and Jourde again appealed to the under-governor of the bank, the Marquis de Ploeuc. (Thiers had summoned the bank's governor to Versailles.) As "men who want the triumph of the Republic at any cost," Varlin and Jourde made clear that "Starving the Parisian population . . . will disarm no one. It will only push the masses to massacres and devastation. We want to avoid these evils; the Bank can help us."[38] Under an unmistakable threat, the Bank of France walked a tenuous line. On the one hand, it supported an insurgent government it opposed, while on the other hand, it effectively kept at bay the violent appropriation it continued to fear throughout the revolution. As bank regent Baron Alphonse de Rothschild (the wealthy banker evoked by the speaker in the Club Saint-Éloi) expressed regarding the bank's decision to work with the Commune, "Each day won is a considerable prize."[39]

Varlin and Jourde's urgency to pay the National Guard reflected the dire economic conditions under which working-class Parisians lived, and the importance the Commune government placed on ameliorating those circumstances. Despite the decree halting the sale of goods left in the Mont de Piété, many of the most vital items—like mattresses, clothing, work tools, and cooking pots—remained unclaimed. Their owners lacked the funds to retrieve even basic items. On April 24 Augustin Avrial, Internationalist and member of the Commune minority, formally proposed that any item valued under 50 francs "can be reclaimed without payment . . .

by only the original owners of the objects." He argued that "We must show that we care about the people, those who made the revolution of March 18. . . . They have the right to have their suffering taken into account." Expanding his point, he insisted, "The institution of the Mont de Piété must disappear." Fellow minoritarian and Internationalist Gustave Lefrançais supported Avrial's proposal regarding goods valued below 50 francs but urged caution about terminating the exploitative institution before establishing something to replace it. "If the Commune triumphs, which is certain," Lefrançais contended, "everything now called Public Assistance—the poor hospital, relief homes, Mont de Piété—will surely disappear. But these correspond to a series of new economic institutions that we still need to create."[40] While deeply flawed, the existing Public Assistance institutions did provide minimal aid to the poor. Subsequent Commune Council discussion emphasized the importance of backing up the symbolic with the practical. Dramatically shuttering the Mont de Piété would demonstrate the Commune's contempt for this form of poor "assistance," but it would also remove one of the few sources of cash for the poor. In a practical vein, Jourde warned that the Finance Commission could not cover all the proposed costs of Avrial's proposition, and ultimately the Commune Council compromised. They passed a measure allowing the retrieval at no cost of any item valued under 20, rather than 50, francs.

During the April 24 debate, Jourde added an additional cautionary note: "Destroying the Mont de Piété would be an infringement on private property, which we have not yet done."[41] Since the French Revolution, socialists and revolutionaries had debated questions of private property ownership. Among their concerns, they queried whether "property is theft," as Pierre-Joseph Proudhon argued; the morality and legitimacy of private property ownership; the class-based nature of property ownership; and how property ownership allowed the creation of new wealth.[42] It became a contested issue during the Commune.

On April 16, the Commune Council had passed a decree that workshops and factories owned by Parisians who had abandoned the city, "people fleeing their civic duty without taking into account the interest of workers," could be seized due to the "cowardly desertion" of their proprietors, whose actions had "jeopardized the workers' lives."[43] The measure penalized proprietors whose flight from Paris left employees without work. Yet it also respected private property, setting up specific legal parameters and restrictions under which the Commune could seize these establishments. Simultaneously, the decree did propound a revolutionary goal: "to establish the practical conditions to promptly put into operation these ateliers, no longer by the deserters who had abandoned them, but by a cooperative workers association."[44] It established a framework for workers to control their own labor, and to do so cooperatively. Under the authority of the Commune's Commission of Labor and Exchange, led by Léo Frankel, it also chipped away at property rights.

That same week, Elisabeth Dmitrieff, a twenty-year-old Russian socialist feminist and member of the International, created a women's labor association. The Union des femmes developed as one of the most extensive, structured, and effective organizations during the Commune. It strove to fundamentally change not only work, but also working women's lives. Developing and implementing a transformative model for all workers, the Union des femmes envisioned the creation of a viable alternative to capitalist production that could ultimately be implemented internationally. In doing so they combined ideals, plans, and practical actions. With sections in most of Paris's arrondissements, and the establishment of a Federated Chamber of Working Women with representatives from every female trade, the Union des femmes infused Paris. The organization's full name, the Union of Women for the Defense of Paris and Aid to the Wounded, presented one of its two immediate goals: defending the revolution. The other was finding nonexploitative work for women. In the long run, they strove to give women control over their labor through the establishment of producer-owned cooperatives. The Union des femmes exemplifies the creative, pragmatic practices that emerged during the Commune, creating a new economic world that revolution allowed.

2.2. Elisabeth Dmitrieff at age eighteen in St. Petersburg.

On April 11, Dmitrieff issued an initial "Appeal to the Women Citizens of Paris," declaring, "Paris is blockaded! Paris is bombarded! . . . To arms! The nation is in danger!" Posted on walls across the city and printed in most Commune newspapers, the "Appeal" asked "Is it the foreigner who has come to invade France? . . . No, these enemies, these assassins of the people and of liberty are French! . . . Our foes are the privileged of the current social order, all those who have always lived from our sweat, who have fattened themselves from our poverty." Dmitrieff made clear this was a class, not an international war: French forces in the service of French elites were attacking working-class French citizens. She termed it a "vertiginous fratricide." Highlighting the global significance of the conflict, Dmitrieff asserted, "all the civilized people have their eyes on Paris, awaiting our triumph so they, too, can deliver themselves." An internationalist thinker, Dmitrieff insisted that Paris was not alone. The "Appeal" highlighted class-based hostilities occurring in Germany, Russia, Ireland, Poland, Spain, Italy, England, and Austria. Linking working-class commonalities across borders, Dmitrieff concluded, "these perpetual clashes between the reigning classes and the people, do they not indicate that the tree of liberty, fertilized by the streams of blood spilled over the centuries, has finally borne fruit?" The violence and oppression suffered by workers across Europe over many centuries was finally coming to fruition in the Commune. Evoking Parisian women's revolutionary legacy, she summoned the *citoyennes* of Paris, "descendants of the women of the Great Revolution," to join her, "To prepare ourselves to defend and avenge our brothers!"[45]

Dmitrieff's politics emerged from her experiences in St. Petersburg, Geneva, and London, and a combination of ideological influences including Russian feminist populism that advocated cooperatives, and Marxist centralization of authority and political action. The daughter of an unmarried Russian aristocrat and a German nurse, Dmitrieff received an excellent education and was raised in considerable comfort. Although her father recognized her and her siblings as heirs, he never took steps to remove their legal status of "illegitimate."

At the age of sixteen, Dmitrieff traveled to Geneva, Switzerland, to study, since Russia barred women from university attendance. There she cofounded a Russian-émigré branch of the International, subsequently journeying to London as the branch's representative to the General Council of the International, where she worked closely with Karl Marx. Impressed with her intellect and abilities, Marx asked Dmitrieff to go to Paris as his eyes and ears when the Commune erupted.

Dmitrieff chose to stay in Paris and take part in the revolution. She established the Union des femmes as an expansive yet highly centralized organization with a top-down decision-making structure.[46] The Union asked support from the Commune's Executive Council, underscoring the importance of the government "addressing the legitimate demands of the entire population, without distinction of sex." Focusing on the pervasive marginalization of women's labor, Dmitrieff argued that elites relied on this intergender conflict as a divide-and-conquer approach. By recognizing and valuing women's labor, the Commune would be undermining the "antagonism on which the governing classes maintain their privilege."[47] To surmount that dominance, the "Appeal" contended, the Commune needed the Union des femmes, and the Union des femmes needed assistance from the Commune government.

The Commune government did aid and support the organization. Unlike the somewhat antagonistic relationship between the revolutionary government and the grassroots, radically democratic women's political clubs, the hierarchical and structured Union des femmes developed a working relationship with the revolutionary administration, particularly with Frankel's Commission of Labor and Exchange.

Frankel, a twenty-eight-year-old Hungarian member of the International and son of a Jewish doctor, had come to Paris in 1867 to complete his apprenticeship as a jeweler. Engaged in leftist politics, Frankel served as a correspondent to a German socialist newspaper and joined the Paris branch of the International, which led to his 1870 arrest under the Empire. Freed by the September 4 declaration of the republic, Frankel actively participated in agitation against the Government of National Defense, spoke frequently at the Club de la Reine Blanche during the Prussian siege, and became a member of the republican Committee of the Twenty Arrondissements. Subsequently elected to the Commune Council, as delegate to the Commission of Labor and Exchange he had promoted the decree allowing the takeover of abandoned ateliers. With the support of Varlin and Malon, Frankel and the Commission also ended night shifts for bakers, arguing for the right of these workers to "return to a normal life," not one where they "never see the day."[48] Facing intense opposition from bakery owners, and a heated debate in the Commune Council, Frankel dramatically proclaimed, "When we make social reforms, do we first consult the bosses? No. Were the bosses consulted in '92? No. . . . I have accepted no other mandate than to defend the proletariat, and when a measure is just, I accept it and I execute it without needing to consult the bosses."[49] The Council broke into applause, and the measure passed.

Committed to bettering the lives of workers by creating a more egalitarian society, Frankel worked to upend existing power hierarchies. On March 30, he wrote to Marx, "If we are able to radically change social relations, the Revolution of March 18 will be the most productive revolution in history." For Frankel, this meant putting economic control into workers' hands. Along with Dmitrieff—also a multilingual foreigner—Frankel was one of the few Communards influenced by Marx, whose works had not yet been translated into French. Each maintained a personal relationship with the political philosopher. Frankel held another distinction as one of the era's few socialist men—with the notable exceptions of Varlin, Malon, and anarchist geographer Élisée Reclus—to recognize and attempt to ameliorate gender inequities. Together these positions made him receptive to the Union des femmes' requests.

The women's labor organization subsequently called on the Commission of Labor and Exchange to charge them with "the reorganization and redistribution of women's labor in Paris."[50] This restructuring would "assure the product to the producer . . . to finally allow workers control over their own affairs." To do so, the Union des femmes identified six areas key to transforming female labor and laboring females' lives. First, avoiding the relentless repetition of movement so common to manual labor, and so "fatal to the body and brain"; second, reducing work hours, since physical exhaustion "leads inevitably to the extinction of the moral

2.3. Léo Frankel. Universal History Archive/Universal Images Group via Getty Images.

faculties"; third, the "annihilation of all competition between workers of the two sexes, their interests are absolutely identical, and their solidarity is vital"; fourth, equal pay for equal work for men and women; fifth, that all participants become members of the International; and finally, a Commune government loan. To undertake this fundamental, sweeping reconceptualization and reorganization in the midst of a civil war, the Union des femmes asked the Commission to extend them credit to cover expenses, one of the most significant being the takeover of "factories and workshops abandoned by the bourgeoisie."[51] Seizing on the Commune's decree on abandoned workshops, Dmitrieff and the Union des femmes acted to address the enormous immediate need for women's employment. In identifying the long-term inequities and exploitation of laboring women, they turned economic and social theory into practice while striving to improve the conditions of working women's lives. Over one thousand *communardes* joined the Union des femmes.

The Union des femmes underscored that while all workers suffered exploitation, women experienced it doubly: as both workers and women. The era's bourgeois ideal placed women in the home, the private or domestic sphere, and men in the public world, laboring for wages. Despite this in no way being working-class reality—working-class women worked—male socialists and labor organizations, often influenced by Proudhonian ideas, embraced these prejudices. As a report from the 1867 Congress of the International in Lausanne, Switzerland, concluded, "we are opposed to women's work in industry . . . women's salary causes men's salary to be lowered." Women consistently received significantly lower salaries than men, something Internationalists and many other male laborers and unions blamed on women, rather than employers. The widespread assumption that most women had a man supporting them financially provided a rationale for women's wages being considered "supplemental." In reality, many women supported themselves and entire households, struggling to do so because a "woman's wage" generally fell below subsistence levels. Proudhonian socialists asserted misogynistic conceptions of

2.4. "Appeal to Women Workers," May 18, 1871, Union des femmes. Wikimedia Commons.

women as unfit for paid work, as the International's Lausanne Congress report continued: "Woman, by her physical and moral nature, is naturally called to the peaceable minutiae of the domestic hearth. . . . We do not believe it is useful for society to give her any other charge." Despite these persistent attitudes, which contributed to women's economic marginalization and impoverishment, working-class women, like men, needed to work.

Questions of female labor consistently intersected with issues of gender-based morality and propriety. The dominant belief that women "naturally" belonged in the private sphere was highlighted by the French term for prostitute: *fille publique,* "public girl." If a proper woman naturally belonged in the private realm, that made those in public improper and unnatural. Concern with propriety and women's sexuality permeated the dominant culture. Prostitution had not been illegal in the period before the Commune; laws and a Morality Police division of the Prefecture of Police had regulated prostitution in Paris under the Empire. While the city allowed sex work in "houses of tolerance," street walking—considered a more "common" form of prostitution—was banned. The Commune government had no consistent policy toward sex work. Some, like the Commune Council delegates from the fourteenth arrondissement, declared, "prostitution on the public way . . . is a permanent cause of demoralization, an attack on morality, and an incessant appeal to the most vile passions." These Council members linked male public intoxication with female street walking, calling for the arrest of perpetrators of both.[52]

The eleventh arrondissement took a different stance. Rather than morally condemning sex workers, the delegates of the eleventh arrondissement—a heart of Parisian working-class life—addressed its root causes. "The lack of instruction and of work, the general cause of the loss of so many women, is without any doubt due to a vicious social mechanism. Thus, the new society must continue the healing. . . . The intelligent organization of women's work is the single remedy for prostitution."[53] Recognizing and addressing the economic and social nature of sex work, the delegates asserted that education and the reorganization of women's labor would "remedy" the prostitution problem. The Union des femmes, headquartered in the eleventh arrondissement, likely influenced the delegates in their recognition of the gendered economic realities of prostitution. As Louise Michel (who was not a Union des femmes member) later wrote in her memoirs, "We shower them with shame because we made them into prostitutes, as if the shame was due the victims and not the assassins."[54] The society and its institutions, not the woman selling her body, should bear the blame. The eleventh arrondissement even likened prostitution to the slave trade. In a decree ending the legality of registered brothels, the "houses of tolerance," delegates described how in the United States, before the Civil War outlawed slave ownership, "the slave trade was prohibited, and slave traders faced severe punishment." The delegates then equated registered Parisian prostitutes with enslaved Blacks, affirming that under the Commune, "one must recognize the commercial exploitation of human creatures by other human creatures." They thus declared that "houses of tolerance," which traded in women, must be banned as a first step to eradicating this form of human exploitation.[55]

While the Commune represented a range of socialist, anarchist, and socialist feminist positions, with various and often conflicting visions of revolutionary change, they all sought to end economic exploitation. Whether critiquing and attempting to change economic relations from above or below, whether through radical action or legalistic measures, Communards strove to create a new and more equitable world. As Louise Michel clarified, "The citizens of France found themselves facing two programs: the first, that of the royalists of Versailles . . . was slavery in perpetuity; the suffocation of intelligence and of justice. The other . . . was the people as masters of their own destinies; the right to live in work; to break the tyrant's scepter under the worker's hammer."[56] The Commune presented Parisians the potential to center the economic world on the power of labor. But it also meant choosing a larger freedom, one in which "intelligence and . . . justice" thrived. The Commune's promise of a full, free life wove together the political realm, economic power, and the flowering of society and culture. Its triumph,

Michel averred, would mean a "peace" where "the laborer returned to his plow, the artist to their brushes, the worker to his atelier, and the earth became fertile again."[57]

Sociocultural

On April 6, Gustave Courbet, painter, sculptor, and member of the Commune Council, issued an "appeal to all artists," calling on "their intelligence, their sentiment," and reminding them "Paris has nourished them as a mother and has given them their genius." Encouraging artists to recognize the ways in which the cultural fecundity of Paris had enriched them, Courbet then addressed both the wartime stifling of the arts, and their importance to the new society. He declared, "At this hour, the artists must (it is a debt of honor) compete to re-establish the arts, which are its fortune. Consequently, it is urgent that we reopen the museums and to think seriously about the next exhibition."[58] Entreating all artists to join together, Courbet called for the formation of a citywide Artists Federation, one that would simultaneously link artists to each other, while sustaining art in the revolutionary city. Their April 14 organizational meeting attracted four hundred artists, an "absolutely full" Medical School amphitheater at the renowned Sorbonne University (the medical faculty had all fled Paris.).[59] Eugène Pottier, designer and poet (and signatory of the eleventh arrondissement's decree outlawing brothels), headed the committee that prepared a manifesto for the Artists Federation. It highlighted "The free expansion of art, unencumbered by any government tutelage or privileges." Reacting against the tight governmental controls under the Second Empire that limited access to resources, to exhibitions, and to the right to call oneself an "artist," the Artists Federation committed to "the independence and dignity of all artists." To attain this, they established an elected committee charged with "fortifying the links of solidarity and achieving unity of action."[60] Like the Union des femmes, the Artists Federation sought freedom of production for its members, creating a system of broad-based mutual support by connecting them in a citywide federation. Courbet's group, like Dmitrieff's, brought together those skilled in many differing *métiers*, what he termed "all the artistic intelligences."

The Artists Federation's elected committee included painters, sculptors, architects, engravers, and "ten members representing the decorative arts, improperly named 'industrial arts.'" In addition to Courbet, other prominent painters included Honoré Daumier, Jean-Baptiste-Camille Corot, and Edouard Manet (Manet was elected, but was not a Communard and never participated). Incorporating decorative artists demonstrated the Artists Federation's rejection of the distinction between fine and decorative arts, a categorization that marginalized and minimized the latter group as not "real" artists, including woodworkers, cabinetmakers, and cobblers.[61] Inspired by egalitarian socialist politics, and by the legacy of the French Revolutionary artists' associations established by painters Jacques-Louis David in 1790 and Eugène Delacroix in 1848, Pottier and Courbet created the Artists Federation as a political project to democratize the elite and elitist, state-controlled art world.[62] On the one hand, this meant significantly expanding the circle of those who could call themselves artists. On the other, it meant bringing art to the people, removing class barriers to artistic exposure and production. The Artists Federation manifesto concluded by committing to "contributing to the inauguration of communal luxury, and to the splendors of the future." Art, beauty, aesthetic pleasures—"luxury" and "splendor" historically guarded within the realm of elite experience—would now be liberated and democratized.[63]

Journalist Henri Bellenger wrote in the Commune newspaper *Le Vengeur,* "A person who works with tools must be able to write a book, to write it with passion, with talent, without feeling obligated to abandon . . . the workbench. An artisan must be able to relax from his daily labor with the arts, letters, or sciences, without ceasing to be a producer."[64] Refusing to accept the age-old division between physical labor and the life of the mind, Bellenger argued that intellectual or artistic enjoyment, or creation, must be accessible to workers. More specifically, he contended that engaging in intellectual or "high cultural" endeavors had to be normalized for workers; it must become part of what it meant to be an artisan. Elements of this push toward egalitarian sociocultural life included the reopening of museums such as the Louvre, free of charge, under the authority of the Artists Federation, as well as the reopening and "radical reorganization" of the National Library, directed by ethnographer, writer, and Commune Council member Élie Reclus (brother of anarchist geographer Élisée). Reclus worked to conserve and protect the library's collections, recognizing their cultural and intellectual value.[65] Physically, he had several National Guard members posted around the building, "fully confident in the Parisian National Guard who, even without having had the occasion to open a single book from the immense collection, are not any less proud that their city possesses such a marvelous ensemble of incomparable documents."[66] In an effort to understand and manage the holdings, Reclus sought help from the institution's librarians and functionaries, most of whom refused to cooperate. An ethnographer and writer, but nonetheless a wartime political appointee with no library credentials or experience, Reclus took seriously his post as National Library director.[67] Cognizant of the historical import of documenting the revolution, Reclus ensured that the National Library's archives received and began to catalogue the Commune's "historical documents, posters, proclamations, and decrees."[68]

Along with the Commune's inspector of municipal libraries, typographer, journalist, and historian Benjamin Gastineau, Reclus worked to make libraries accessible and responsible to the public. As Gastineau wrote, "Under the Second Empire, public libraries—just like everything else—were pillaged. The privileged carved out their own libraries from the national libraries, borrowing books and rarely returning them, thus depriving workers of the most necessary and useful works." Gastineau condemned elite Parisians' abuse and destruction of public libraries, which he likened to their pillaging of "everything else." Underscoring how their theft of books kept important texts out of workers' hands, Gastineau exemplified the Commune's focus on the intellectual lives of everyday

Parisians. Similarly, Edouard Vaillant, the Commune's education delegate, castigated limitations to museum access as being "under a monarchical regime" where "a visit to collections" was a "privilege." "Under the communal regime," he stated, "every gallery, library, collection, etc., must be opened widely to the public. The desire to read and to study must be sufficient to open the doors."[69]

This idea of open doors, of equal access to spaces and artifacts and elements of what had long been conceived as "high culture," as the province of elites, embodied the luxury promised by the Artists Federation, a central tenet of this "communal regime." As Michel later recalled, "Courses were opened everywhere, responding to the eagerness of youth. We wanted everything at once: arts, sciences, literature, discovery, the flamboyant life. We hurried to escape the old world."[70] Just as Varlin and other artisans had taken night courses after full workdays under the late Empire, the idea of the right to rich, multifaceted lives developed from mid-nineteenth-century socialisms and labor movements. It exploded into praxis in the new world emerging under the Commune. As Courbet wrote to his parents in an April letter, "Paris is a true paradise."[71]

Education played a fundamental role in developing this new world. The Commune had inherited a gender-segregated, class-based instructional system run by the Catholic Church. In the aftermath of the 1848 Revolution, Louis-Napoléon's Falloux Law gave the Church authority over education, as a conservative reaction against the insurgency. Thiers (then part of Louis-Napoléon's government) argued that parish priests should control primary education: "I am counting on them to spread that true philosophy that man is here to suffer."[72] Pedagogical goals tended toward servility rather than intellectual development. Girls received instruction primarily from nuns. While lay teachers needed a certificate to prove their training, nuns required only a letter of obedience from their supervisors. As an 1870 Paris school district report on women teachers observed, "their knowledge and teaching ability leave something to be desired, but they are morally superior, more tactful, and more devoted."[73] The Second Empire used education as a political tool, one to maintain the socioeconomic status quo, reinforcing hierarchies of gender, class, and religion. In 1870, on the eve of the Commune, 84 percent of Parisian primary schools were private, and approximately one-third of children attended no school.[74] Neither free nor mandatory, schooling lay out of the reach of most poor people, and it provided minimal instruction to those who did attend. Substantive education remained the privilege of the wealthy, and almost exclusively of men.

Months before the beginning of the Commune, André Léo wrote, "The partisans of women's equality . . . have come to understand this truth. Their primary objective must be the free school, a school of reason and liberty."[75] She aimed to break away from the existing instruction girls received, which stressed domesticity and taught them subservience and piety. Léo had long promoted the importance of egalitarian and secular girls' education as the "primary objective" of feminists. Education could bring the ability to understand, and ultimately to access, power. This explains conservative elites' jealous hold on instruction, as well as the Commune's elevation of it—for children, for workers, through formal structure, and through cultural institutions like museums, libraries, and theater.

The Commune's educational plan emerged from decades of socialist and feminist pedagogical theorization, centered on the idea of "integral education." A term introduced by the utopian socialist Charles Fourier in 1829, integral education advocated an intellectual, physical, practical, equal, and universal program. Henri Bellenger's contention that a person should be capable of artfully writing a book while remaining strongly identified as a worker reflected the ideal of integral education. A student should be able to "earn a living, while simultaneously developing his spirit through study and thought."[76] Practical and intellectual training for all citizens, regardless of gender or class, formed its base.

Anticlericalism also constituted a core element of the Commune's reconceptualization and reorganization of education. It too emerged from the era's socialist and feminist movements. The Commune Council decree separating Church and state on April 2 had terminated state funding for all ecclesiastical institutions and mandated secular education. The Commune thus established France's first secular public schools.[77] The recognition of the vital importance of education meant that radical pedagogical reform arose from multiple quarters during the Commune. On April 1, a delegation from Education Nouvelle, an organization that formed during the Prussian siege, submitted a proposal to the Commune Council, underscoring the centrality of instruction and asking that "religious or dogmatic instruction . . . be immediately and radically suppressed, for both sexes, in every school." Clearly anticlerical, the statement called for "rational, integral instruction" in place of the faith-based program delivered by the Church. Advising integral education as the "best possible apprenticeship for private, professional, political, and social life," Education Nouvelle asserted that it should "be considered a public service of the first order, and consequently free and complete for all children of both sexes."[78]

The Education Nouvelle proposition called for a "republican education." In labeling schooling a "public service," and using the language of a free and egalitarian "integral education," they made clear their advocacy for a social republic—a republic concerned not just with political equality, but also with social and economic justice. Conservative republicans sought educational reform, including the secularization of schools. But republican socialists also advocated change in instructional methods, contents, and goals.[79] The long-term French debate over what the republic meant and who it served remained a central political contestation.

Three men and three women made up the Education Nouvelle delegation. One of the women, Maria Verdure, the daughter of Commune Council member and schoolteacher Augustin Verdure, also participated in another pedagogical reform organization, the Society of Friends of Education. On their behalf she submitted to the Commune a call for state-funded day care centers. Extending some of the ideas behind Education Nouvelle's proposal, including barring the employment of any "representative of any religion," the day care request outlined the parameters they considered best for both staff and children. Specifying the importance of staff rotating tasks to avoid becoming "sad and gloomy" from repetitive labor, the society emphasized that children must be "only in the care of cheerful and young people, as much as possible." Wearing black was forbidden.[80] Verdure and the Society of Friends of Education carefully outlined a fully secular and (what they understood as) a pleasant environment in which young children and workers would flourish. Similarly, the third arrondissement town council (*mairie*) issued a call for support and reform of an orphanage. Underscoring the importance of sufficient staff and respect for the role of the female instructor, they stated that "teaching is incompatible with the internal administration of an orphanage. Preoccupying teachers with issues of cooking and childcare diminishes the sublime role of instruction."[81] Stressing the value of female teachers' skilled labor, the statement recognized that dominant, sexist ideas about working women would assume they should also fill care roles, even if those tasks fell outside of their professional responsibilities, just because they were women. The appeal also addressed the importance of providing the orphaned children with "free and moral instruction," making sure they were not "isolated from the rest of society."[82] Attention to the social, intellectual, and professional well-being of workers and students reflected the progressive and inclusive philosophy of integral education. It contrasted sharply with most established labor and pedagogical approaches during this era.

The Commune Council appointed from its ranks a nine-member Education Commission on April 1—the same day Education Nouvelle submitted its proposal. Composed of three medical doctors, three teachers (one of whom was Maria Verdure's father Augustin), two journalists, and a sculptor, the Education Commission was charged with "creating a plan to render instruction free, mandatory, and exclusively secular."[83] Almost immediately, four of the nine commission members resigned their positions on the Commune Council (part of an early wave of resignations of elected Commune members with liberal, rather than socialist, politics). With neither leadership, a concrete plan, nor funds, the Commission languished. Establishing a new government, and a new way of governing, in the midst of a civil war, meant that certain aspects of governing received less direct attention. This gap, however, allowed Education Nouvelle to step in.[84] Following the group's April 1 proposal, the Commune Council responded that they were "completely favorable to their suggestions for radical education reform."[85] Education Nouvelle, the Society of Friends of Education, and other grassroots associations, including social welfare and education, thus initiated education reform during the revolution.[86] Like the Union des femmes, these organizations engaged in extragovernmental politics.

The Commune Council re-established the Education Commission and appointed Edouard Vaillant its head on April 20. Facing resistance from some arrondissements, especially regarding the eradication of religion from schools, Vaillant continued relying on local and grassroots initiatives, while simultaneously working toward broader, citywide changes. On May 14, Vaillant announced the reopening of a former drawing academy as the Young Girls Professional School of Industrial Arts, to be directed by *citoyenne* Parpalet, an instructor of sculpting/model-making. The new school would "teach drawing, model-making, wood and ivory sculpture, and the applications of the art of design to industry." Consistent with ideas of integral education, students would take concurrently "courses intended to complete the students' scientific and literary education." The Commune had established a similar school for boys earlier in the month. Yet training young women both professionally and intellectually exemplified the radicalism within the Commune's pedagogical program, as they legitimized women's place in the public spheres of both labor and ideas.[87]

Women emerged as a force in education reforms. Marguerite Tinayre, a teacher and member of the International, became inspector of schools in the twelfth arrondissement, the first woman to hold such a post in Paris. Paule Mink opened a free girls' school in Montmartre; Michel submitted a blueprint for girls' integral education that formed the basis for her later anarchist education programs; and Marie Manière founded a professional school for girls, while also proposing a plan for girls' atelier schools to provide secular, "progressive education entirely removed from prejudice."[88] In the Commune's final days, Vaillant appointed Léo, Anna Korvine-Krukovskaya Jaclard (a member of the Montmartre Women's Vigilance Committee), Marthe-Noémi Reclus (wife of Élie Reclus, and with Léo a member of the 1868 Society for Claiming Women's Rights), Isaure Perrier, and Anna Sapia to form a commission to reorganize and oversee girls' schools. Vaillant and the Education Commission also took the exceptional measure of equalizing the salaries of male and female teachers. While the Commune did not extend gender-based wage parity beyond teachers, compensating women's labor equally with that of men demonstrated a revolutionary step toward the revaluation not only of women's work, but also of women's place in the public sphere.

The Parisian entertainment world, a large and class-stratified set of communities, unsurprisingly responded to the Commune in differing ways. A look at the May 15 Parisian theater listings in the *Journal Officiel* showed the Gymnase Theater announcing that its "administration has very significantly reduced the price of all seats." The Port-Saint-Martin Theater offered "a grand patriotic performance" to raise money for "the families of the wounded and dead of the eleventh arrondissement." And the Gaité was "reopened by the artists reunited as a company."[89] The announcements reflected changes made under the Commune to better include workers by reducing ticket prices, to patriotically support those who had sacrificed for the revolution, and for artists to control their own work cooperatively "as a company."

Popular and classical concerts and a broad range of theatrical performances opened to the wide Parisian public, providing entertainment, cultural enrichment, political platforms, and charitable fundraising opportunities. In early May, the Commune took over the renowned Paris Opera, shuttered since the March 18 uprising. Many of the Opera's musicians had fled Paris or refused to perform under the revolutionary authority, so the Commune delegates filled gaps with performers from other orchestras in the city. On May 12, the musicians and employees met their new director, *citoyen* Eugène Garnier, in the foyer of the National Opera Theater. "Dear artists," he began, "or I could say dear comrades." Garnier then laid out plans to develop a concert series with proceeds split between "victims of war" and the musicians themselves. Appointed by the Commune Council, Garnier proposed a reform project that only vaguely suggested the potential of artists gaining a stake in their performances. He told the musicians and staff that he "hoped that as soon as possible" they would be able to "perhaps realize the dream that we artists have all had . . . of working a bit for ourselves, instead of using our lives and our talent to make a fortune for the directors."[90] In the meantime, controlling the Opera—both the institution and the majestic building—meant appropriating one of the city's most elite and closed cultural institutions. The Commune planned a grand concert with a program departing radically from those of the Second Empire by including contemporary and revolutionary works. But Versailles troops burst into the city the day before the scheduled May 22 Opera performance.

Like the arts and education, journalistic expression found new freedoms under the Commune. An explosion of over ninety newspapers appeared in Paris during the revolution.[91] The vast majority supported the Commune. Advancing a range of leftist politics, they reflected various levels of journalistic professionalism, and employed styles from serious to humorous to bawdy. The extraordinary proliferation of periodicals reflected Parisians' pent-up desire for free expression, the taste of such communication opportunities they had experienced through the lifting of press restrictions and in the public meetings under the late Empire, and the relative ease of access to basic publishing tools. Just as the government and many organizations plastered announcements on walls across the city (as Commune critic Edmond de Goncourt complained, "Posters, posters, everywhere, and then more posters!"), newspapers conveyed fresh information to readers and to listeners—as café-goers often read and discussed the news aloud.

Some papers published only one issue, like the hand-written *Le Drapeau rouge* ("The Red Flag"), "Political, Critical, and Humorous"; or two issues, such as *Le Fédéraliste* appearing May 21 and 22, just as Versailles troops entered the city; or three issues, as with

L'Ouvrier de l'avenir ("The Worker of the Future"), "A Political and Social Newspaper" published at the beginning of the Commune by labor unionists. Commune Council member Auguste Vermorel published *L'Ordre*, attempting to appropriate the term "order" and redefine it as the new egalitarian world of the Commune, rather than the antidemocratic meaning given it by the right. The paper failed after four issues, likely because the title's popular association with Thiers and Versailles repelled Vermorel's desired audience.

Le Prolétaire ("The Proletarian") also numbered only four issues. Edited by the organizers of the eleventh arrondissement Club des Prolétaires in the Commune's final weeks, this radically democratic, anticlerical newspaper opened itself as an egalitarian forum. In its second issue, the editors announced to its readers that the publication "is your work and your intellectual property." One of the club organizers explained that they established the Club des Prolétaires to enable "education of the people by the people." They then created the newspaper of the same name so that "those who cannot explain themselves at the podium, can do so in writing." Encouraging grassroots input and assuring access, they urged "no citizen to hesitate to bring us their contributions, just because they aren't in the habit of writing or don't know how to express themselves correctly, we will make their projects known. . . . It is essential we not lose one single idea that is useful to humanity."[92] Like most political clubs, the paper encouraged and valued popular input. In addition to polemics and news, the periodical published political poems, indicating an editorial openness to varied literary forms. The first, by G. Barthelemy, celebrated the Commune's destruction of the Vendôme Column. Under Courbet's direction, the Commune toppled the iconic 145-foot monument crowned with a statue of Napoléon I, symbolically destroying France's fealty to Napoléon I, militarism, and international aggression. Barthelemy's poem professed "Because we stand for law and honor / We smash the Column."[93] The second poem *Le Prolétaire* printed, "A la Femme" ("To Woman"), by M. Picard, called women to "Rise up—finally stop being a slave." *Le Prolétaire*'s final issue appeared on May 24, likely the last paper to be published under the Commune.

2.5. The toppled statue of Napoleon I by Antoine-Denis Chaudet, formerly atop the Vendôme Column. Roger-Viollet.

The satirical, ribald *Père Duchêne* had one of the larger readerships, printing approximately 70,000 issues per day. A resurrection of a 1790s French Revolutionary paper of the same name, the 1871 version began under the Government of National Defense, which subsequently censored and shut it down. *Père Duchêne* re-emerged early in the Commune. Reviving the bawdy style of its original editor, the far-left revolutionary Jacques Hèbert, the newspaper reflected the intensely anticlerical perspective of its 1871 editors, Maxime Vuillaume, Alphonse Humbert, and Eugène Vermersch, members of the Commune's "majority." These three men, like the editors and publishers of many of the period's most successful papers, sat on the Commune Council. In the first issue printed after March 18, *Père Duchêne* effused, "Vive la Commune, Fucker!" Exalting the new revolution, it explained, "The Commune is simply the city of Paris administering itself, adopting the same measures for all of its children, providing the same aid to all, having the same level of care for all . . . instead of a heap of holy jackasses from arrondissement town halls, finally a good mother instead of the dirty buggers of the government."[94] Grabbing the reader's attention with "Vive la Commune, Fucker!" the article seriously but colorfully explained the stance of the new government. In an exaggerated voice of the "common man," *Père Duchêne* provided both politicized news and entertainment to the Parisian public.

Le Cri du peuple, the most widely read Commune newspaper, published a daily print run of 100,000 copies. Edited by the renowned journalist, author, and Internationalist Jules Vallès, the "daily political newspaper," *Le Cri du peuple* was another of the socialist periodicals censored by the Government of National Defense and reborn (ten days later) under the Commune. In contrast to *Père Duchêne*, Vallès and *Le Cri du peuple* advocated the Commune's moderate "minority" position. The majority/minority split had come to a head over the establishment of the Committee of Public Safety, the extrajudicial arm of the Commune created on May 1. *Le Cri du peuple* published the minority's May 15 declaration condemning the Committee, insisting that "The Paris Commune has abdicated its power into the hands of a dictatorship, to which it has given the name Committee of Public Safety."[95] Signed by Vallès, Varlin, Frankel, Gustave Courbet, and the nineteen other minoritarians, the statement asserted their anti-authoritarian opposition to the majority's antidemocratic moves. Less than four weeks earlier, *Le Cri du peuple* had published a "Déclaration de la Commune de Paris au peuple français," articulating the Commune's program and affirming it as a direct democracy, in which the people possessed "the right of permanent control," including the right to revoke the position of any and all elected or appointed members of the government.[96] The Committee of Public Safety undercut that authority and sovereignty of the people.

In April, the Commune began suppressing right wing, anti-Communard newspapers. Though some journalists welcomed the move, André Léo protested. Castigating the censorship sponsored by the Commune's majority, Léo wrote in *La Sociale*, the newspaper she co-edited, "If we act like our adversaries, how will the world choose between them and us?" Léo did not hesitate to condemn the

Commune government when it took undemocratic or sexist measures. Refuting its censorship act, she insisted, "freedom of thought must be inviolable."[97] Because of her involvement, *La Sociale* published more feminist journalism than any other Commune newspaper. Drawing on her pre-Commune feminist advocacy for the expansion of women's sphere and the implementation of mandatory secular education, while building on her renown as a novelist and political writer, Léo used the pages of *La Sociale* (and to a lesser extent *La Commune* and *Le Cri du peuple*) to press the Commune to centrally involve women in the development and operation of the egalitarian new world. She encountered mixed results. Arguing that radical change could not succeed without women, she blamed France's past revolutionary failures on women's ongoing marginalization. Léo expressed anger that the Commune risked repeating the error: when a woman offers "her devotion to this Revolution which has forgotten her, she is rejected with insult and contempt!"[98]

Here Léo referred specifically to women's battlefield participation. As Louise Michel clarified, on the battlefield, "The armies of the Commune include female battlefield cooks, nurses, and soldiers."[99] Within the city walls, *communardes* formed vigilance committees that searched for and arrested military deserters. Many women's clubs, including the Federated Legion of Women, the Daughters of *Père Duchêne,* and the Club of Women Patriots, prepared to defend Paris and ultimately to fight on the barricades. Both Léo and Michel claimed women's right to battlefield participation. In an April 12 *La Sociale* article titled "All Women with All Men," Léo argued "women, like men, naturally participate there."[100] Though they primarily fed and nursed soldiers (both traditionally female roles), the women nonetheless faced hostility for trespassing in a distinctly male sphere. The Commune's Committee of Public Safety outlawed women on the battlefield on May 1. This measure, passed on the day of the committee's establishment, indicated the antifeminism of the majority faction. Mere rules, however, did not stop devoted *communardes*. Rank-and-file soldiers welcomed the women on the front lines. But the predominantly working-class women faced opposition and "brutal insults" from the Commune army's officers and surgeons, as Léo explained in *La Sociale* on May 9. These elite men expressed a "bourgeois and authoritarian mindset" indicative of their gender and class privilege, and their conception of who "belonged" on the battlefield.[101]

The Final Days

The battlefield moved increasingly closer to Paris, until the two became one. Versailles had put the city under siege beginning in April, Paris's second such blockade within a year. Now instead of the Prussian army, hostile French forces encircled the capital, increasingly tightening their grip. By mid-May, the military situation appeared increasingly dire. Tensions continued to swell. An early Commune rout had led to the capture and summary execution of Communard leaders Emile Duval (head of the Ex-Prefecture of Police) and Gustave Flourens, despite the Geneva Convention of 1864's ban on killing prisoners. In response, the Commune arrested and held as hostages the archbishop of Paris, Georges Darboy, and dozens of other ecclesiastics. The Commune Council offered Thiers a hostage exchange: the archbishop and seventy-four other prisoners in trade for Blanqui, who Versailles had arrested on the eve of the Commune. Thiers refused on May 11. Political and military pressures neared eruption.

Symbolist poet Auguste Villiers de L'Isle Adam commented that in May, "Paris is fighting and singing! Paris is about to be attacked by a ruthless and furious army and she laughs!"[102] In what became the Commune's final weeks, the city continued to celebrate its freedom, despite the unceasing hostility. Neighborhoods held concerts and fairs. During April, Paris successfully held its annual Ham Festival, undeterred by the ongoing civil war. The Commune undertook symbolic, triumphant demolitions, including formally burning a guillotine to clearly reject that violent legacy of the Great Revolution, "cheered by an immense crowd." In May they ceremoniously destroyed Thiers's house, and days later demolished Napoléon's commemorative Vendôme Column. Each event drew huge, enthusiastic audiences, reveling in their conquest of despotism.[103] Explaining the surprising situation of mid–civil war Paris, Danish writer Wilhelm Dineson observed, "Happily, the city was not like what those outside imagined it to be. Shops, cafés, and restaurants were open, you could find the usual quantities of merchandise and food at normal prices . . . the streets were cleaned and illuminated, and while few theaters were open, other distractions were available every day: clubs in churches, concerts in gardens, in the Tuileries, for example."[104] The final of four Tuileries concerts, the May 21 event, in which thousands of Parisians celebrated the revolution with abundant food, drink, and music in the red flag–bedecked Tuileries Palace, embodied the essence of the Commune. Having appropriated once royal property, the insurgents opened the opulent space. Inverting hierarchies, erasing barriers, the Commune released the pleasures of body and mind, once held jealously by elites, to the people of Paris.

3

Explosion

"In the supreme struggle which began 48 hours ago, the Parisian population has given all of its energy," reported the Commune's *Journal Officiel*. "Children build barricades that their fathers defend, and the women, the mothers, rifles in hand, sustain citizens' courage with their words and actions." Highlighting Communard women's bravery and fortitude, the newspaper described how a "battalion of Montmartre women took fire from Versailles regiments for four hours, defending several barricades—which they had built themselves—until National Guard reinforcements finally arrived. We saw several of these patriotic women gravely wounded."[1] Walking to meet his compatriots that day, Élie Reclus recounted seeing young boys building a barricade. "What the children accomplished was truly astonishing. Two or three boys worked together to loosen a paving stone, which a child of five or six then carried, sagging under its weight. Lads perched on a wall acted as masons and architects. All of these school-escapees were happy and proud to play—and that is the word—their role in the civil war."[2] Two days after Versailles troops stormed Paris on Sunday, May 21, Communard men, women, and children supported the Parisian National Guard, acting as a grassroots supplemental force, defending their neighborhoods, devoting themselves to preserving their city and their revolution.

May 21 to 28 became known as "Bloody Week," seven days of brutal urban conflict and ruthless slaughter by the Versailles army.

Instigated by intense anti-Communard and anti-Paris propaganda, the mostly provincial Versailles soldiers killed with a stunning virulence. Thiers and his military leaders not only allowed the bloodbath, but they had also set up a framework to facilitate it. Even once the Commune's resistance lay broken and beaten, the systematic massacre continued into June.[3] By viciously crushing the insurgency, the French state intended to go beyond ending the uprising to also send a message. Terrified and enraged by radical and working-class Parisian appropriation of political authority and inversion of the city's economic and sociocultural hierarchies, Thiers's government continued their punishment and retribution, executing, imprisoning, and exiling thousands more Communards.

As Versailles troops swept into the city, Communards activated defense plans they had created but hoped to never use. The Commune Council met at the Hôtel de Ville on the morning of Monday, May 22. Their subsequent proclamation declared, "To the People of Paris, To the National Guard. . . . The hour of the revolutionary war has arrived. . . . To arms! Citizens, to arms!"[4] They issued a *levée en masse*, calling for a "mass rising" against the enemy. This conscripted all able bodies into the military, just as Revolutionary leaders had done in 1793 in response to invasion and internal crisis. Paris faced a Versailles army of 130,000; the Commune had barely 20,000 soldiers.[5]

Vigilance committees, political clubs, the Union des femmes, and other neighborhood organizations rose to the occasion. The "battalion of Montmartre women" discussed in the *Journal Officiel* referred to the Montmartre Women's Vigilance Committee, which included Louise Michel, Nathalie Lemel (the bookbinder and operator with Varlin of the free kitchen La Marmite), Anna Korvine-Krukovskaya Jaclard (member with Léo on the Commune's commission on girls' education), and Béatrix Euvrie Excoffon (vice president of the Club Boule-Noir). Vigilance committees had first been developed during the Prussian siege, established to support the defense of the city. They re-emerged during the Commune, fulfilling a range of community needs including defense, and, according to Michel, "leaving no one without shelter or bread."

3.1. Paris Commune, 1871. Barricade at the Hôtel de Ville (4th arrondissement). Roger-Viollet.

Montmartre had two of these organizations, one for men and one for women. A participant in both, Michel suggested that "perhaps they will be blended, because no one worried about which sex one belonged to in order to do one's duty."[6] An idealized assessment, as only in the Commune's final days, as the French National Army swarmed Paris, did such an absence of gender roles and barriers become something of a reality.

After spending fifteen days serving in a battlefield hospital at the Fort d'Issy, Beatrix Excoffon returned to Paris "for the Vigilance Committee . . . where we had to organize all of the aid to the wounded, send out battlefield nurses, etc." Composed primarily of *clubistes*, these neighborhood voluntary organizations provided vital medical support and provisions to the Parisian National Guard. Maintaining a battlefield hospital at the Elysée Montmartre concert hall, the group also "sent deputations to burials, took care of the widows, mothers, and children of those who died for liberty."[7] They adhered to an ethic of community support as the violence and losses mounted. As a women's vigilance committee, they retained traditionally female roles in the care work they provided. Yet, as their neighborhoods became combat zones, they began to build barricades, take up arms, and fight the invading enemy.

W. Pembroke Fetridge, an American writer and publisher living in Paris, observed that the Committee of Public Safety called for the erection of "barricades in every direction. . . . Women and children worked just as actively as the National Guards themselves."[8] Fetridge related seeing many women come to the Hôtel de Ville "who wished to take their part in the defense. At one time thirty women came with a demand for a *mitrailleuse* [machine gun] to arm the barricade in the Place du Palais-Royale. They all wore a band of crape [*sic*] round the left arm; each one had lost a husband, a lover, a son, or a brother, whom she had sworn to avenge." Emphasizing the women's determination and vengeance, Fetridge continued, "Horses being at this time scarce in the service of the Commune, the women harnessed themselves to the enormous machine, and dragged it off, fastening their skirts round their waists lest they should prove an impediment to their march. Others followed bearing the caissons filled with munitions. The last carried the flag." Jules Vallès, Commune Council minority member and editor of *Le Cri du peuple,* presented the women with the *mitrailleuse* flag, and "an order written and signed by Delescluze, commissioning the above mentioned *citoyennes* to aid in the defense of Paris."[9] Charles Delescluze, a long-time socialist journalist, veteran of 1848, and former Devil's Island political prisoner, was a Committee of Public Safety member and head of the Commune military. In intentionally selecting a civilian for this position, the revolutionary government sought to mitigate potential military abuses of power. Delescluze and the Commune included these *citoyennes* by officially authorizing their role "in the defense of Paris," a role they chose themselves. This exemplified the reciprocity between the government and the people that rested at the heart of Commune ideology.

After the women left the Hôtel de Ville "bearing with them the engine of destruction," a group of teachers arrived, offering "to employ the children under their charge in making linen bags necessary for the barricades, that they might also have their glorious part in the defense of Paris." The educators received an authorization "to transform their schools into workshops," and the children they enrolled would "receive rations of food and wine," just as National Guard members did.[10] This enactment of the levée en masse meant mutual support between the Commune and its citizens: men, women, old, and young.

Like the students sewing sandbags, and the boys Élie Reclus witnessed constructing a barricade, children participated in various aspects of the Commune's defense. Versailles arrested 651 Communards aged eighteen or less; the number of youths who participated and died during the insurgency remains unknown.[11] While the National Guard did not recruit fighters under seventeen years old, boys did manage to enter their ranks. Some joined as a family with their fathers and brothers, and some Guard units allowed boys without parents or economic support to join. Particular divisions accepted children more broadly. The 1st Battalion of the National Guard included eight boys between ages twelve and sixteen, and both the Avengers of Flourens (named in memory of the Commune Council member captured and summarily executed by Versailles early in the conflict) and Turcos battalions incorporated fifteen- and sixteen-year-olds. The Pupils of the Commune consisted only of boys aged eleven to sixteen, nearly all from the working-class neighborhood of Belleville.[12] Beyond these somewhat formal affiliations, in the final, desperate days, even more young people joined relatives and neighbors on the barricades. They fought to save their lives, families, community, and the promise of the Commune.

The majority of Paris's working class lived on the Right Bank, the north side of the River Seine. Versailles troops entered the city from the south, via the Left Bank, confident of facing minimal resistance from the mostly anti-Communard elite inhabitants. Working to hold the city center, National Guard battalions, including the 6th Battalion, led by Varlin, quickly constructed barricades to prevent further Versailles advances. Varlin worked in coordination with Polish revolutionary and military strategist Walery

Wroblewski, who attempted to convince the Commune leadership to shift all its military strength to the Left Bank, anticipating Versailles's plan of attack. Delescluze refused.[13] Wroblewski had correctly assessed Versailles's strategy, but, as historian Frank Jellinek clarified, "Wroblewski was not a Parisian" and thus did not comprehend the depth of neighborhood loyalty among its citizens. Communard and journalist Prosper-Olivier Lissagaray later explained that "the heart of a revolution cannot be displaced for military purposes."[14] Delescluze had understood that the Parisian forces would not abandon their neighborhoods during an assault on the city, that community provided the core of their military organization and political and social lives. By midweek, facing relentless onslaught and losses, Commune leaders ordered National Guardsmen to defend their neighborhoods, a widespread move that had already begun.[15]

The Union des femmes also readied for the barricades, living up to its full name: the Union of Women for the Defense of Paris and Aid to the Wounded. Earlier in May, the organization had issued a "Manifesto of the Central Committee of the Union des femmes" that underscored their militancy and battle-readiness. An "anonymous group of reactionaries" had published and widely posted a statement allegedly on behalf of "the women of Paris." It called on "the generosity of Versailles and asked for peace at any price." The Union des femmes responded viscerally. Enraged by the suggestion of Versailles possessing generosity, they countered, "the generosity of cowardly assassins!" Eviscerating the statement, the "Manifesto" continued, "No, it is not peace, but all-out war that the working women of Paris claim! Today conciliation would be treason! . . . The women of Paris will prove to France and to the world that they will also know, at the moment of supreme danger— on the barricades, on the ramparts of Paris, if the reactionaries force the gates—to give as their brothers their blood and their life for the defense and triumph of the Commune, that is to say the people!"[16] When that "moment of supreme danger" arrived later that month, the women of the Union des femmes followed through. On Thursday, May 25, Dmitrieff issued her final message to the members:

"Gather all of the women and the committee members and go immediately to the barricades."[17]

Barricades of various sizes, composition, and strength arose across the city, concentrated especially in working-class areas, but Paris's newly built wide boulevards proved difficult to blockade—as intended by Louis-Napoléon and his urban planners when they redesigned much of the city in the 1860s. Additionally, Versailles troops rarely attacked barricades head on. They instead approached from nearby streets, infiltrated adjacent buildings, and shot down at the blockades from above.[18] Taking and holding nearby structures became vital for defense. As retribution, the Committee of Public Safety issued an order on May 22 to burn down any house from which Versailles soldiers had fired shots.

During Bloody Week, Paris burned. The Committee of Public Safety order contributed to the inferno, but the first major building set aflame during the conflict was the Ministry of Finance, ignited by Versailles's incendiary shells. Buildings exploded under Versailles mortars, their machine gun barrages set structures alight, and they also intentionally lit fires. The Commune, too, used flames to block advancing enemy troops. The extent to which the citywide blazes resulted from their strategic efforts remains unclear, as by midweek the revolutionary government had little control over its combatants. But the Commune government did set fire to buildings representing power, wealth, and control of the city. Once the revolution had opened access to these halls and all that they symbolized to the people of Paris, surrendering them appeared untenable. As defeat became increasingly inevitable under the brutal onslaught, destruction became a viable wartime option.[19]

Incendiary directives came from both sides of the majority/minority governmental divide. Théophile Ferré, the Committee of Public Safety member in charge of the Committee of General Security, and a close friend of Michel, ordered the Ministry of Finance, the Prefecture of Police, and the Palace of Justice set ablaze. As the Commune government abandoned the Hôtel de Ville on May 24, minority Commune Council member Jean-Louis Pindy, an anarchist, Internationalist, and the building's governor, instructed the National Guard to burn it. Pindy thought this would cover the Commune leaders' tracks as they relocated to the eleventh arrondissement, the revolutionary stronghold in the midst of working-class Paris.[20] The Committee of Public Safety torched the Palais-Royal, and the Commune's General Bergeret gave the command to ignite the Tuileries Palace "after all of the hangings had been soaked in petrol and barrels of gunpowder had been stacked at the foot of the grand staircase."[21] Malon described the inferno: "The palace of kings rose up like a volcano, with a terrible noise . . . a black cloud filled the sky, obscuring the air," and the justification for it: "The people of Paris . . . being massacred at that moment for their republican and socialist faith . . . had the right to burn the palace of kings."[22] The Louvre library burned, but Gustave Courbet protected the museum and its art from incineration. As a multiday conflagration engulfed Paris, poet Augustine-Malvina Blanchecotte, who termed Communards "the ignorant masses," climbed to the top floor of her neighbor's house to survey the city: "But what a representation of hell! What an incomparable sight . . . fireworks of bombardment in the frenzy of its fury, with . . . the thunder of explosions to the north, to the south, near, far, everywhere, next to us, below us, in all directions, illuminated by flaming houses."[23] Louis Gallet, writer and opera librettist, woke on the morning of May 25, witnessing: "Paris burns! In the immense circle of the horizon before us, the somber city is crowned in a mane of fire."[24]

Fire also had historic and symbolic resonance. Clarifying that he "did not become an incendiary without having taken a good look at the past, without having sought out my ancestors," Vallès compared himself and his comrades to heroic historical figures who burned warring cities in the ancient world. Communards likening themselves to such classical forebears incensed the Parisian bourgeoisie.[25]

Gendered Repression

While the hierarchy-inverting goals of the Commune intensified long-held antisocialist antagonisms and generated fear and hatred on the part of conservative France, Versailles and its sympathizers also expressed deep enmity toward activist women. This hostility took many forms, most infamously portraying *communardes* as frenzied arsonists solely responsible for the city's fires. The myth of the *pétroleuse*, the working-class Parisian female incendiary, spread globally and became intractable. The immensity and drama of the fires drew international attention, and the uncertainty of who bore responsibility for igniting them led to widespread speculation and accusations. Working-class *communardes* made ideal targets, as their participation in politics and warfare—in some cases their mere presence in a city turned battlefield—defined the threat of disorder. Since they had already stepped outside of the bounds of what the bourgeoisie considered acceptable female behavior, why, in a time of desperate crisis, would they not go further?

The myth had a specific focus: *pétroleuses* allegedly lit fires in Parisian neighborhoods already occupied by Versailles. Conservative newspapers contributed to the mounting hysteria, as *Le Gaulois* described in detail the "mixture of kerosene, tallow, and sulfur" the *pétroleuses* used;[26] *Paris-Journal* reported on thirteen young women arrested and shot for throwing petrol into basements; and *Le Figaro* told of a woman and a little girl guilty of carrying a milk bottle filled with kerosene (*pétrole*), which they had allegedly poured into basements. The typical work of women and children, transporting liquids and goods in bottles or boxes, became demonized and criminalized. It led to their arrests or (more often) immediate executions. People living in Versailles-controlled areas blockaded their basement windows and doors in fear of female arsonists. Rumors spread that the Commune paid ten francs for each building burned; both the U.S. ambassador to France, Elihu B. Washburne, and Versailles military officer Eugène Hennebert, wrote in their memoirs that eight thousand women did this work; Hennebert termed them "an army of furies."[27]

Not all anti-Communards accepted the myth of the *pétroleuse*, however. Maxime du Camp, a conservative writer and critic of revolutionary men and women, contended "Paris was taken by madness . . . this legend . . . was absolutely false."[28] He quoted

3.2. Caricature of the Commune as a *pétroleuse* burning Paris. "La Commune, numéro 35." Musée Carnavalet/Roger-Viollet.

American diplomat Colonel Hoffmann, who termed "ridiculous that bands of women prowled the streets, throwing *pétrole* into basements and setting them on fire." "Kerosene," he wrote, "is the madness of the moment." Historian Edith Thomas, in her groundbreaking 1963 book *Les Pétroleuses*, analyzed the cases against the eight women tried and convicted as *pétroleuses*, confirming the fictional nature of both the specific charges and the larger myth.[29] However, she simultaneously asserted the possibility that *communardes* did participate in burning Paris. Thomas pointed to Article 14 of the Union des femmes's "Statutes": "The sums that remain after administration costs will be utilized . . . to purchase *pétrole* and arms for *citoyennes* fighting on the barricades," but clarified that we have no evidence they used the kerosene.[30] Communards undoubtedly employed fire as a weapon of war, the details of which remain unclear. Female combatants fought shoulder-to-shoulder with their male comrades during Bloody Week. Identifying the *pétroleuse* as a sexist, classist, and ultimately deadly fabrication does not preclude recognizing the possibility that both male and female Communards participated in battlefield incendiarism.

Women built and defended barricades alongside men and children across the city.[31] They played an integral role in the urban armed conflict. A barricade at the Place Blanche, just below the Montmartre Cemetery, had what was likely the largest concentration of female combatants. A reporter for the *Journal Officiel* wrote how on the night of May 22 he encountered a barricade "perfectly constructed and defended by a battalion of around one hundred and twenty women." Immediately, "a black shape stepped out of the shadows. . . . It was a young girl wearing a revolutionary cap, rifle in hand, ammunition belt across her chest." The *citoyenne* demanded his papers, then let him pass.[32] The newspaper *Le Rappel* told of "a company composed of only *citoyennes*, nearly all armed with rifles," and both Sutter-Laumann and Michel recalled red flag–bearing bands of *communardes* passing through this neighborhood, making a notable presence.[33]

Building and fighting on barricades to defend the revolution and its promises of equity and freedom, *communardes* carried on the nearly century-long tradition of insurgent Parisian women. Versailles's official report to the Minister of War, however, portrayed them as "completely ignorant and lacking any sense of morality."[34] Prepared by Captain Briot, the report concluded that women were fooled or enticed into participating in the uprising. Explaining that the battlefield cooks "follow the insurgent troops without knowing what they were doing," the report claimed that they, and "the battlefield nurses, the barricade fighters . . . All of these women . . . receive their instructions and orders from the Central Committee of the Union des femmes . . . under the authority of Mademoiselle Demitrieff [sic]." The authorities attributed all women's insurgent activism to one mastermind woman (a Russian), finding it incomprehensible that so many working-class women intentionally became revolutionaries. Denying women's agency and political consciousness, the Versailles report lumped together all *communardes,* unable or unwilling to recognize their range of feminist, socialist, and/or anarchist politics. As Briot's document concluded, the reasons "women were drawn to the revolutionary movement [were] . . . : living in concubinage [cohabitation outside of marriage], demoralization, and debauchery." In his telling, women's uncontrolled, irrational sexuality, their "thirst for pleasures unknown and ardently desired," drove them, rather than a desire for equity and liberation.[35] A combination of immorality, lust, and irrationally thus drew women to the revolution, according to the Minister of War report, and once involved, their weakness led them all to fall under the sway of Russian Elisabeth Dmitrieff. Rampant right-wing fear that foreigners instigated and perpetuated the insurgency intensified when the foreigner was female.

Other critics of the Commune similarly assessed and sexualized *communardes.* Maxime du Camp wrote, "They had tossed off more than their bonnets . . . they dropped all of their clothes."[36] Rather than seeking citizenship and equality, as they professed, their actual goal and "secret dream . . . was having multiple men." The renowned writer Emile Zola, also a Commune opponent, similarly denigrated activist women. Pronouncing that a *communarde* carrying a rifle "has more coquetry than political passion," he maintained that women considered the gun merely an alluring accessory, one that would "without a doubt make other *citoyennes* jealous of the martial allure of battlefield cooks."[37] Zola expressed even greater hostility toward *les raisonneuses*, "women who reason," insisting "one must flee from this type of political woman, as one does from the plague." Women who presumed intellectual or political authority posed the greatest threat for Zola. Where women on the battlefield appropriated a particular type of masculine space, *raisonneuses* trespassed in a male realm of greater significance: that of politics and ideas. The suggestion of female political leaders particularly infuriated him.

He termed the Commune's socialist feminist leadership "a sort of feminine Central Committee," an idea which he found completely absurd. Disparaging Communard women did double duty for Zola in simultaneously criticizing male Communards. From the bourgeois perspective, such women lived improper and immoral lives even when politics were discounted, merely by working and operating in the male, public world. Interlaced with bourgeois male fears of an inversion of class and gender hierarchies, *communardes* threatened to turn their world upside down.

"It Will Serve as a Lesson"

"Versailles turned every district it took into a slaughterhouse," charged Michel.[38] From its entry into the city, Thiers's army killed both systematically and wantonly. The *New York Times* reported Thiers pledging "that it was the determination of the government to punish the perpetrators without mercy."[39] As they moved into neighborhoods and over barricades, Versailles soldiers rarely took prisoners. They shot them instead. Manifold accounts and recollections tell of the slaughter. Thiers's men captured the Saint-Forentin barricade, killed the thirty surviving National Guardsmen, and threw their bodies in a ditch. Nearly three hundred Guardsmen sought sanctuary in the Madeleine Church; Versailles fighters entered the church and shot them.[40] Having blackened hands could lead to arrest or execution for suspicion of using gunpowder, as could carrying a bottle or tin, which could be used to carry *pétrole*. Geneviève Breton, a young bourgeois woman working with the International Red Cross, recorded in her journal, "Outside of our windows, they arrested individuals and without judgment shot them behind the barricade! . . . I expressed my indignation to the soldiers several times, but they were so enflamed that they heard nothing."[41]

National Guardsman Charles Sutter-Laumann recalled how "The cadavers of executed Guardsmen were lying on the sidewalks in seas of blood. They were everywhere."[42] Blanchecotte wrote about the construction and defense of a barricade on her street, of the horror of Paris burning, the terrifying sounds of bombs and guns, and finally of emerging from the shelter of her house to see "blood everywhere, filling the doorway, covering the sidewalk, even the gutter was red; the ground littered with pieces of bayonets, scraps of belts, parts of tunics, pieces of blouses, caps, cartridge belts, shoes."[43] Songwriter, journalist, and Commune Council member Jean-Baptiste Clément explained the political motivation behind the fratricidal bloodletting: "the bourgeois killed on the spot, not so much to kill men as to kill an idea. 1871 laid out clearly the principle of class struggle."[44] From the perspective of Thiers and the National Assembly, the Commune had to be crushed in a way that obliterated not only the revolutionary movement itself, but also the concepts and ideals behind it. The repression had to make the possibility of a resurrection or imitation unthinkable.

At times, even death proved inadequate. Only defilement would suffice. Commune Council member Maxime Vuillaume passed a defeated barricade on the Place Saint-Michel, in the city center, where "a dozen cadavers stretched out on the ground, faces muddy and bleeding. Between their lips, icy with death, someone had put the mouths of bottles and pipes . . . such a disgrace!"[45] Demeaning slain Communards reflected the ways in which Versailles dehumanized their enemy.

The French military often conjoined sexual violence with murder. Lissagaray related how thirteen women were shot on the Place Vendôme "after having been publicly outraged." He clarified: "there were rapes at multiple points during the raids. Young riflemen on the Boulevard Voltaire bragged about it *in front of us* . . . and in *front of us* recounted all of the details."[46] Lissagaray noted the widespread use of rape to conquer the Parisian populace, as the soldiers' blatant boasting of their crimes made clear. Jules Bergeret, a member of the Central Committee of the National Guard, reported that women arrested in the first, eighth, and ninth arrondissements were brought to the Place Vendôme and "stripped, raped, and massacred."[47] Georges Jeanneret, a member of the Commune's Ex-Prefecture of Police, described how after Versailles soldiers shot female prisoners, "they stripped them, as they lay dying . . . sometimes the offenses went further, as at the bottom of Montmartre and at the Place Vendôme, where women were left naked and defiled."[48]

The Committee of Public Safety's first revolutionary trial debated whether the Commune should kill ten hostages as reprisal for Versailles's rape and murder of a battlefield nurse. For the court members, the sexual attack elevated the murder to be "in violation of all human laws."[49] An often unacknowledged but pervasive tool of war, rape functioned as a way to debase the enemy, specifically humiliating and violating women. It served as a brutal punishment to women who had not only stepped out of their socially prescribed passive gender roles but who had also challenged the political hierarchy. Because of the era's dominant idea that women "belonged" to men, sexually violating women also meant attacking enemy men's property. No published history has yet investigated the extent and use of sexual violence by the conquering French army.[50]

Immediately after entering Paris, Versailles had established courts-martial to rapidly try and convict insurgents. A decree passed by the Government of National Defense during the Prussian siege had legitimated this system of military justice, at least in times of war. Allowing neither legal representation nor appeals, the courts found nearly all prisoners guilty. Some arrestees received brief trials lasting mere minutes, while others met instantaneous arbitrary conviction. The condemned faced immediate execution by firing squad or a forced ten-mile march to prisons in the town of Versailles.

Twenty such military courts operated across Paris, including at the Châtelet Theater, in the Luxembourg Gardens, and on the Place Vendôme.[51] Iconic places of luxury occupied by the Commune, Versailles reclaimed them through summary justice and mass executions. One court-martial operated at La Roquette prison, outside of which a crowd had ceremoniously burned a guillotine in early April, symbolizing the Commune's rejection of the bloodletting associated with that part of the French Revolution. Writer and politician Camille Pelletan told the story of a teacher mistakenly arrested in a Versailles sweep and taken to La Roquette prison. "A battalion chief stood at the entry, sizing up the arrivals, then barking 'To the right! To the left!'"[52] Sent to the left, guards ordered the teacher, "Put your things in this sack. We're going to shoot you, scoundrel!" Pelletan clarified that "To the right! To the left! was how justice was rendered," not only at La Roquette, but also the other major courts-martial. A guard ultimately realized the teacher had official papers, which meant prison rather than death. "There was soon a crowd of prisoners, three thousand in his estimation. All Sunday, all night, the gunshot blasts did not cease." Forced by a sergeant the next morning to "Pick up the bastards and put them in the horse carts," the teacher relayed that he hesitated when "it seemed that several of those shot still breathed. But the soldiers shouted, 'keep going!' We gathered 1,907 bodies." Confirming that his informant had not exaggerated, Pelletan quoted the conservative newspaper *Liberté*'s matter-of-fact reporting that more than four thousand National Guard prisoners appeared before "a martial court installed at La Roquette. A police commissioner and some police security agents were charged with the first screening. Those designated to be shot were directed inside. They shot them from behind as they walked in, then threw their cadavers on a pile."[53] On May 25, as battles still raged, Thiers issued a triumphal statement: "The soil of Paris is inundated with blood and strewn with insurgent corpses. . . . It will serve as a lesson."[54]

Like the teacher mistakenly arrested on the street, legions of working-class Parisians faced similar experiences, often with worse consequences, as national troops took over more of the city.

Sutter-Laumann lamented the dehumanization of the innumerable prisoners still being brought in front of the courts-martial, "The barracks were packed with prisoners who had been shot ten by ten. . . . In the Parc Monceau they were executed in batches." Detainees unable to keep up with the others on marches to courtsmartials or prison, "the old, wounded, and sick," were helped along by their comrades, but if they fell, "a bullet from a revolver ended their suffering."[55] As groups of bourgeois Parisians returned to the city once the Commune's defeat appeared imminent, they verbally and physically attacked the condemned on their prison treks. Sutter-Laumann described these elite men and women as a "despicable and stupid mob, massed on the sidewalks [they] overwhelmed the vanquished with insults and threw stones at them."[56]

In the days before Versailles entered Paris, Thiers had rejected a torrent of requests to trade the imprisoned Blanqui for the archbishop of Paris and other Commune hostages. Despite pleas made by the American ambassador, the papal nuncio, the lord mayor of London, and the archbishop himself, Thiers said no. According to Élie Reclus, Thiers refused "under the pretext that freeing Blanqui would give the insurrection a too-dangerous leader."[57] More likely, allowing the Commune to continue to imprison the archbishop and five other priests benefited Thiers by further blackening the image of the revolutionaries in the eyes of the world.

After hostage exchange negotiations failed, the majority Blanquist-dominated Committee of Public Safety pushed for the execution of the prisoners, while the minority, anti-authoritarian associationist socialists, ardently resisted. Thiers's army pushed through the city, rapidly nearing the La Roquette prison that held Archbishop Darboy and the other hostages, forcing a decision. Under pressure from the enemy army and an aggressive, anticlerical crowd outside the prison, the Commune held an impromptu court-martial on May 24. Found guilty and condemned to death as reprisal for Versailles's many summary executions, the archbishop and five other priests immediately faced a firing squad. The Blanquist Ferré, who had long supported killing the hostages, including advocating it at a meeting of the Club de la Révolution, signed the death warrant.[58] Two days later, as French national troops advanced, Commune losses and deaths skyrocketed, and the Commune government disintegrated, approximately fifty more priests and spies were shot to death in the Commune's name. In what became known as the Massacre on the Haxo Road, a large and hostile crowd demanded the execution of these prisoners. Varlin and Vallès, both from the minority, and Frédéric Cournet, a majoritarian Blanquist, were among the Commune members intensely and passionately opposing the executions. Ultimately, Blanquist Commune Colonel Émile Gois gave the order to shoot.[59] This deed cemented the image of the Communards as bloodthirsty "savages," vengeful and murderous to their prisoners. Victor Hugo's poem on Paris's "Terrible Year" further popularized the vengeance taken for the event: "Bandits have killed sixty-four hostages, / We strike back by killing six thousand prisoners. / We cry for the first, we scoff at the last."[60] Despite Versailles slaughtering one hundred times more people than did the Commune (and the true numbers of dead Communards likely exceeded by several times Hugo's estimate), the world largely mourned the loss of the Versailles dead while justifying the slaying of Communards.

On Saturday night, May 27, French army troops smashed through the gates of the walled Père Lachaise Cemetery, one of the last holdouts of Communard fighters. After brutal battles among the tombs, Versailles soldiers seized the surviving defeated opponents, lined them up against the wall, and opened fire, gunning down 147 people. Nearby, Varlin and Ferré continued to fight that Sunday morning, escaping as their barricade near the Chateau d'Eau was taken. At rue Ramponneau and at rue de la Fontaine-au-Roi, the Commune's final barricades fell.

Defeat

Communards fled Paris to avoid arrest or assassination. With Thiers in power, bourgeois and other sympathetic Parisians denounced the revolutionaries, and some attacked them in mobs. The police received an astonishing 399,000 denunciations, as people used the opportunity to settle a variety of related and unrelated scores. Placed under martial law, the defeated city's streets filled with military regiments. The Prussian army, still outside of the French capital, cooperated with Thiers to block Communards' flight.

Varlin did not attempt to flee. The afternoon of the downfall, a priest saw him sitting in a café and reported him to a nearby officer. Arrested and marched to Montmartre by six guards, a growing and increasingly angry crowd followed, blaming Varlin for the archbishop's death (which he had opposed) and shouting "Death! Death!" The enraged mob demanded he be shot at the spot where, on March 18, the two generals were gunned down as the insurgency began. Beaten by the soldiers and the throng, bloodied and blinded, he managed to shout "Vive la Commune!" as the soldiers fired a fatal volley.[61] In the words of Vallès, one of his primary adversaries in the Commune Council, Varlin was "the most remarkable personality of the Commune. . . . He was the soul of every strike, of every protest . . . a man of great modesty."[62] He was thirty-one years old.

André Léo, Léo Frankel, and Elisabeth Dmitrieff managed to escape Paris. Léo, like other fortunate revolutionaries, first hid at the home of an ally. She left Paris in late July on a false passport created by Geneva-based engraver and Internationalist Adhémar Schwitzguébel and smuggled to her through her socialist network. Arriving in Basel, Switzerland, she joined her partner Malon, and immediately began speaking and writing about her Commune experience. Dmitrieff and Frankel fled together in late June. Both wounded defending a barricade in the eleventh arrondissement, Dmitrieff had saved the more gravely injured Frankel. Each recovered in safe houses in Paris. Multilingual and educated, the Russian-born Dmitrieff and Hungarian-born Frankel slipped out of the city, posing as a German-speaking bourgeois Prussian couple traveling to Switzerland by train. Within months the twenty-year-old Dmitrieff had returned to Russia and abandoned her nom de guerre (Dmitrieva was her grandmother's surname; Elisabeth took the masculine form Dmitrieff). By reverting to her legal name, Elisabeth Tomonovskaia, she made Elisabeth Dmitrieff, the woman hunted by French police for "incitement of civil war," disappear.[63] Frankel, aged twenty-seven, left Switzerland for London in August. He continued his socialist journalism and involvement with the International there until 1875, then in Hungary until 1889, when he ultimately returned to Paris. These three Communard refugees, and innumerable others, found safe havens in Switzerland and England because—along with Belgium—these countries refused France's extradition requests. Maintaining Thiers's categorizations of the Communards as criminals, not revolutionaries, Versailles insisted that the insurgency "must not be confused with a political act," and thus asked countries to deny its participants asylum and instead extradite them to France to face trial.

Théophile Ferré eluded capture for two months. In July, after relentless searches, including arresting and ultimately releasing several men they mistook for Ferré, the Versailles agents invaded his parents' house. Finding his mother and extremely ill, bedridden sister Marie, the military police pressed his mother to surrender the whereabouts of her son. Michel, close friends with both Marie and Théophile, recounted that the mother's dogged refusals led the investigators to threaten, "If you won't tell us where your son is, we're going to take your daughter." Their unyielding insistence on taking Marie from her sickbed proved intolerable to the older woman. "Madame Ferré collapsed . . . she lost her reason, speaking incoherent phrases. . . . In her delirium the unhappy mother let escape the words 'rue Saint-Sauveur.'"[64] Versailles agents thus found and arrested Ferré. His mother died eight days later in the Saint Anne Asylum. Sentenced to death on September 3, the government executed Ferré on November 28.[65] He was twenty-five years old.

Military police arrested Louise Michel's mother Marianne Michel in late May, using her to bait her revolutionary daughter. As soon as she heard, Michel rushed to the Montmartre military stronghold Bastion 37 and offered herself in exchange for her mother's freedom, a trade eagerly granted. Herded with other prisoners to a destination unknown to them, Michel witnessed arrestees being shot and the struggles of the wounded, weak, and aged. The captured were marched to the military encampment Satory

3.3. Théophile Ferré, several days before his execution. Courtesy of The Charles Deering McCormick Library of University Archives and Special Collections, Northwestern University.

within the town of Versailles, where a crowd descended on them, "howling like a band of wolves; some shot at us and my comrade had her jaw broken."[66] The *New York Daily News* reported on the "horrible" behavior of these crowds, shouting at people being marched to captivity, "Shoot the wretches! Show them no mercy!"[67]

Arriving at the Satory prison camp in a torrential downpour, Michel encountered her Montmartre Vigilance Committee comrade Beatrix Excoffon, who had for the past four nights "slept in the courtyard on the cobblestones." People filled every inch of the overcrowded and filthy prison. Excoffon later wrote, "Louise arrived with dripping clothes. . . . I wrung them out on her back, and since I had a pair of stockings in my pocket, I gave them to her." Michel resisted taking the stockings because she felt certain she would "be shot the next morning." Soldiers had informed her of plans for her immediate execution.

The women had not been searched as they entered the prison, but they foresaw an inevitable inspection. Michel carried incriminating documents, including "an order to remove one of the small organs from Notre Dame and transport it for singing lessons at her school." When a female prison worker asked them for their papers, Excoffon "responded that I had none." Then, "in silence, the seven of us began to chew the papers, which was not a small enterprise." By the time the police lieutenant arrived to confiscate their documents, "they were no longer recognizable."[68]

Thiers's government formally arrested approximately forty thousand people, driving them on foot from Paris to overflowing formal and makeshift prisons around Versailles, including military base outbuildings, cellars, open fields, and the stables of the Saint-Cyr military school. Satory had only one water source for prisoners, a pond in which the wounded washed themselves. A woman incarcerated there told Lissagaray, "Thirst tormented us so cruelly that some of us rinsed our mouths with the bloody water."[69] Lacking sufficient space near Versailles to hold the Communards until trial, the government shipped nearly half the arrestees over one hundred miles to France's west coast, holding them for months in prison ships and military forts under fetid conditions.[70]

After being moved from Satory to Chantiers to Versailles prisons, Michel faced trial before the Sixth Council of War on December 16, 1871. Making no apologies, asking no forgiveness or mercy, and refusing legal counsel, Michel accepted responsibility for things she did, such as carrying a gun, wearing a military uniform, and "seeking to overthrow the government." She confessed to incendiarism, saying she tried "to create a barrier of flame to block the invading Versailles," and that she did so with no accomplices, and she did not challenge multiple erroneous accusations, including that she had organized the Central Committee of the Union des femmes (which was actually Dmitrieff's project). Attempting to deflect blame from her corevolutionists, Michel accepted responsibility for everything. Two weeks after the state put to death her friend and ally Ferré, and in the wake of the violent loss of innumerable comrades and the destruction of her revolutionary hopes, Michel responded to the trauma with an embrace of martyrdom. When the Council of War returned from deliberations and unanimously condemned her to deportation to a "fortified enclosure," she replied, "I would prefer death."[71]

Instead, the government deported her and 4,500 other convicted insurgents (only twenty-five of whom were women) to its prison colony in the South Pacific archipelago of New Caledonia.[72] After enduring months, or in some cases years, in French prisons, deportees spent the four-month sea voyage to New Caledonia housed in large shipboard cages. Many conservatives had labeled Communards savage, animalistic, and uncivilized. The official "Parliamentary Inquest of the Insurrection of March 18" termed the revolutionaries "new barbarians," and warned against the "return of savage acts that afflicted us and dishonored us in the eyes of the world."[73] For the government, exiling the insurgents to distant, tropical New Caledonia would thus serve four interlinked purposes. First, it would rid France of these uncivilized "barbarians" by banishing them over ten thousand miles away. Second, the authorities hoped that many of the deported Communards would ultimately choose to remain as colonists on the islands after they completed their sentences. France began to significantly expand its empire in this period, so expelling the revolutionaries meant both increasing colonization and reducing the number of returning undesirables. Third, national leaders believed that surviving in the "natural," undeveloped, and "uncivilized" New Caledonian world would eventually civilize the immoral working-class Parisians through intimate contact with the laws of nature and God. Finally, the government considered New Caledonia's indigenous Kanak people to be the most savage and least civilized of their colonial subjects. By inserting the white Communards among the Black Kanak, French authorities hoped that the increasingly civilized Europeans would help bring civilization to the Indigenous people. Class, racial, and imperial motives together underpinned the deportation scheme.[74]

In New Caledonia, most Commune veterans lived in huts under harsh conditions on a rural island peninsula, a "prison without walls," guarded at the only end connected to the mainland; others lived in prison barracks. The majority of deportees remained aloof from the Indigenous population. After decades of French colonial oppression, appropriation, and violence, the Kanak staged an anti-imperial uprising in 1878. In response, most Commune veterans sided with France—the same government that had massacred their families and allies and extinguished their revolution. Racial alliances trumped those of class. Michel stood as an exception. The only Communard to consistently support the Kanak through their insurgency, she had developed relationships with Kanak and had worked with an Indigenous man to translate, transcribe, and publish their oral tales, striving to counter France's interpretation of the Kanak as cultureless and savage.

The Commune had damaged the widespread image of France as the epitome of civilization. Newspapers across the globe—from London to New York to Sydney to Mexico City—had breathlessly apprised their readers of Paris in flames and awash in blood. Stunned by stories and images of the internationally renowned capital set ablaze, many world newspapers denounced the brutality with which Versailles eviscerated the uprising. Yet most condemned the Communards for the arson and the insurgency.[75]

Théophile Gautier described the Communards as "wild beasts, stinking beasts, venomous beasts . . . monsters of the heart, with deformed souls," who lived in subterranean zoos where one day the "Beastmaster" neglected to lock "the doors of the menagerie, and the ferocious animals spread through the terrified city, howling savagely."[76] Typical of portrayals by a broad range of anti-Communards, these animalistic metaphors reinforced images of working-class Parisians as not only savage, but also subhuman. Augustine-Malvina Blanchecotte similarly rendered them as "wild beasts [who] only resemble humans by their form. They are monsters who should be classified under zoology. They are not men."[77] Such dehumanization reflected the propaganda disseminated by Versailles during the revolution. When Thiers pulled his army out of the city on March 18, he had done so with the intent of bringing in provincial troops, recognizing the widespread anti-Parisian sentiment beyond the capital. Constructing one's enemy as devoid of humanity, civilization, and morals, as "ferocious" and "monsters," makes slaughtering them not only palatable, but also righteous. A method typically used in class-, race-, ethnicity-, and religious-based violent oppressions or population "cleansings," Thiers and French conservatives did this with Communards.

Approximately one thousand Versailles troops perished battling the Commune. The French military records named and identified almost all of their soldiers killed. But they were unsystematic in tracking the number of Communard deaths, in part to conceal their own culpability. Thus, the extent of revolutionary casualties remains contested even now. Sixty-six years after the fall of the Commune, left-wing scholars such as Frank Jellinek estimated deaths as high as 30,000.[78] More recently, conservative historian Robert Tombs has argued for a revised number between 6,500 and 7,500 official deaths, relying on documentary evidence from official government and military sources.[79] In recent decades, most historians have agreed on a range between 17,000 and 25,000, based on a broad array of sources including government reports, qualitative and quantitative population analyses, and firsthand accounts.[80]

Resurrection

Despite the French national government's extreme efforts to eradicate even the memory of the insurgency, the Commune left a long and intricate global legacy. Contestation over the meaning and significance of the revolution, as well as what comprised the event itself, began before the final barricade fell. Its drama, violence, and intense polarization drew an extraordinary level of international attention, fueling fears on the right that Communes would rise up in other cities, as they had done across France and in Algeria. The ominous specter of the Commune lurked beneath class relations, especially in the world's ever-growing urban spaces. For the left, the liberatory hope of the insurrection burned brightly, though often tempered by the threat of ferocious state repression. Embracing the memory of the Commune as a model for collective, emancipatory movements provided a beacon, showing the potentiality of such revolutions at any time in any city. These oppositions and possibilities have marked political landscapes to this day, in France, its colonies, and in moments of citizen and subject rebellion across the globe.

In the immediate aftermath of the insurgency and its repression, French conservatives worked to shape the Third Republic, the national government established with the fall of the Second Empire. Most surviving leftists remained imprisoned in France, incarcerated in the New Caledonian penal colony, or exiled in Switzerland, England, Belgium, or the United States. They could not return to France due to outstanding arrest warrants, or because Versailles had tried and sentenced them in absentia. Antidemocratic and monarchist politicians punished Paris. The national government once again rescinded the capital's right to an elected mayor, something denied for nearly one hundred years before, and again for over one hundred years after, the Commune. The Third Republic kept the city under martial law until 1876, disbanded the National Guard, and rebuilt Paris to erase the traces of the Commune. The Catholic Church, still the official church of France, constructed the enormous white Basilica of Sacre-Coeur to crown Montmartre. It appropriated substantial working-class space and loomed over the neighborhood, becoming a major visual point on the Parisian skyline. Sacre-Coeur manifested the Church and state's efforts to assert their combined power, to demonstrate their triumph, and to insist on working-class atonement. Symbolically, the massive basilica represented the victory of the party of "moral order" and the Church over the people of Paris.

The survival of the republic remained tenuous throughout the 1870s as republicans vied with monarchists for power. By the end of the decade, the royalists lost influence as republicans came to dominate the legislature, including not only the conservative republicans who had supported Thiers but also increasing numbers of moderate and left republicans. The question of an amnesty for Communards, debated and dismissed since 1871, finally became a possibility. Victor Hugo, the first and most persistent amnesty advocate, upheld the importance of reconciliation, vilifying the destructiveness of allowing national divisions to fester. Lamenting the futility of civil war, he wrote:

Why! On one side France, and on the other side France!
Stop! Your success brings only mourning.[81]

A partial amnesty was passed in 1879; on July 11, 1880, France extended a general amnesty. While some Communards had received pardons earlier, this law freed those still incarcerated, and allowed deportees and exiles to return. On the final leg of Louise Michel's ten-thousand-mile journey home from New Caledonia, where she had spent nearly seven years in the penal colony, thousands of supporters and admirers welcomed her train as it pulled into Paris's St. Lazare station. Earlier that year, on May 23, over twenty thousand people gathered at the Wall of the *Fédérés* (Commune army) in Père Lachaise cemetery, commemorating the slaughter of Bloody Week. Every year since, people have assembled in the same location to remember the Commune and to keep alive the history and ideas of the Communards.

The Commune reached beyond Paris. In its own time, it spurred several simultaneous urban uprisings that expressed solidarity with Paris and shared its revolutionary ideals. In France, contemporaneous Communes arose in cities including Lyon, Narbonne, Dijon, Saint-Etienne, and Marseilles, with the latter's fourteen-day event surviving the longest. Many insurgents sought a federation of Communes across France, autonomous and independent yet linked and cooperative.

While the Paris insurrection inspired other revolts, it arose within a year of insurgencies inspired by radical republican ideals across France and in its colonies. Lyon's March 1871 Commune erupted only months after the city had experienced a September 1870 Commune, an uprising ignited by the September 4 fall of the Second Empire and birth of the republic.[82] Revolutionary republicanism also sparked a September 1870 women-led revolt of Black Martiniquans against white colonists.[83] French colonists in Algiers, Algeria, many of them exiled 1848 revolutionaries, rose up in March 1871 and formed a Commune. These events also coincided with the Indigenous Algerian Kabyle uprising against French imperialism. The white Algerian colonists did not support the Kabyle, nor did they oppose imperialism.[84]

The Commune looked both to the past and to the future. Deeply attached to France's revolutionary legacy, Communards referenced and linked to their revolutionary foremothers and fathers, harkening back to French Revolutionary forms, including establishing political clubs and ultimately a Committee of Public Safety. Yet the Commune also broke new revolutionary ground. The simple fact of time altered even the elements the insurgency mimicked. History influences the future, but it does not and cannot repeat itself. The Commune emerged from socialist and feminist movements and ideas that developed in the long wake of the French Revolution. Communards seized their insurrectionary moment to initiate a range of progressive and radically democratic programs, which many of the insurgents had been intimately involved in developing in previous years, and they did so while immersed in civil war. This alone would provide inspiration to later activists. The brutal realities of the demise of this radical experiment added an epic and near-mythic element to the event. The ruthlessness with which Versailles crushed the uprising made clear the immense threat posed to existing power hierarchies. Not merely the ideas behind the Commune, but also their practices and implementations, provided a template for substantial change, a map to egalitarianism that suggested multiple routes to sketches of differing possible ends. The legacy of the revolution delimits neither the paths to justice, nor the types of justice that could be pursued. Cut down just as it had germinated, grown, and hinted at flowering, the Commune suffered a bitter end. But it did not fail. It persists as a guide to multiple radically democratic goals.

In the century and a half since the 1871 revolt, the Commune has stood as inspiration to a plethora of activists and global movements. In 1879, in Chicago, nearly 60,000 people celebrated the Commune with a "program of singing, dancing, and drilling" organized by the Workingman's Party of Illinois;[85] in 1889 in Alexandria, Egypt, anarchist printers on March 18 marked the "eighteen long years past to the day since the Commune"; in the early twentieth century, anarchist feminists Voltarine de Cleyre and Emma Goldman each credited the Commune as an inspiration; Vladimir Lenin studied and emulated aspects of the Commune in his approaches to revolution in Russia (the Commune flag shrouded his body at his 1929 death); in 1925, the New York Workers' Party of America commemorated the revolutionary anniversary with over 10,000 attendees in Madison Square Garden; in 1927 and again in 1967, workers formed the Shanghai Commune;[86] Occupy Oakland established the "Oakland Commune" in 2011; and in 2020, the artist Banksy funded the "Louise Michel," a refugee rescue ship in the Mediterranean Sea. The Commune is sufficiently capacious to hold all of these and more, past and future, under its liberatory umbrella.

To commemorate the one hundredth anniversary of the Commune in 1971, artist Ernest Pignon-Ernest covered the steps approaching the enormous Basilica Sacre-Coeur with hundreds of larger-than-life screen-printed images of dead bodies (Image 3.4). Pignon-Ernest's work contested the benign image

3.4. Commune—Sacre-Coeur 1971. Ernest Pignon-Ernest. La Commune de Paris, 1971. Screen print. Courtesy Galerie Lelong & Co.

of the monumental white basilica, insisting on the recognition of the site's bloody and punitive history.

The definition and legacy of the Commune remain contentious. A history emphasizing only the government, only the men who occupied the Hôtel de Ville, provides a partial and even distorted vision of the fullness of the event. The Commune operated as a vast orchestra, sometimes harmonious and lovely, often discordantly cacophonous. Political clubs, the Artists Association, vigilance committees, the Union des femmes, National Guard battalions, arrondissement committees, battlefield nurses and cooks, journalists, laborers, teachers, communal restaurants, entertainers, and artisans each played vital roles, contributing to the resonance and reverberation. The women and men of Paris—those remaining in the city—seized the moment to insist on their right to self-creation and self-rule. Laborers saw possibilities of bettering the conditions of their work and lives. Barriers to the right to think, create, and express oneself began falling. Undergirding everything was an idea of radical equality, the ability of a population to reject the hierarchies imposed by the weight of history and to replace them with egalitarianism, argumentation, and the collective construction of a just future. Those seventy-two days in 1871 set a lofty bar and posed a profound threat to the status quo. In all of these ways, the Commune still lives.

Acknowledgments

I wrote this book during a year of pandemic and fiery politics, grateful to escape daily into the optimistic and fascinating world of the Paris Commune. I want to thank series editor and extraordinary Commune scholar Kristin Ross, and Rutgers University Press Director Micah Kleit, for inviting me to take on this project. At Rutgers University Press, Elisabeth Maselli has patiently and expertly helped me navigate the technical aspects of book publishing.

Writing this book felt like coming home. I began thinking and writing about the Paris Commune as an MA student at Northern Illinois University, studying with Harvey Smith and the late William Beik, Margaret George, and Marvin Rosen. My gratitude to these generous and inspirational scholars remains enormous. I wrote my dissertation at UCLA on women in the Commune, guided and motivated by Edward Berenson, Kathryn Norberg, Robert Brenner, Carole Pateman, Ruth Milkman, and John Hatch. As I turned that dissertation into my book *Surmounting the Barricades: Women in the Paris Commune,* I had (and continue to enjoy) exceptional mentoring by Karen Offen, Marilyn Boxer, Elinor Accampo, Laura Levine Frader, and the late Rachel Fuchs. These mentoring relationships all evolved into warm friendships. I am profoundly grateful to these women.

Returning to the Commune after many years, I have drawn on the extensive archival research I conducted for earlier projects. I want to again express my indebtedness to archivists and librarians from whose expertise and time I have benefited: in Paris, at the

Bibliothèque Marguerite Durand (thanks especially to Annie Metz), Bibliothèque Historique de la Ville de Paris, Archives de la Préfecture de la Police, Service Historique de la Défense, Bibliothèque Nationale, and Archives Nationales; in Amsterdam, at the International Institute of Social History, where I am particularly indebted to Mieke Ijzermans, the former information director; and in the Eugene W. Schulkind Paris Commune Archive at the University of Sussex, England. During the past year Beth Kucera, head of interlibrary loans at the University of Wisconsin, Milwaukee, has enabled me to obtain important sources safely and easily despite pandemic conditions.

To my niece and bibliographer Tess Eichner Considine, *mille mercis* and much love for your meticulous work. I want to express my deep gratitude to my sister, Susan Eichner, for once again providing expert and generous editing, as well as for her ongoing "grammar hotline." My parents, Norman Eichner and Corrine Bochan Eichner, are no longer with us, but my love for them and appreciation of their tremendous support remain eternal.

Finally, my loving thanks to Kennan Ferguson for facilitating, encouraging, and collaborating on this book. I could not be more grateful for his superb insights and constructive critiques, his unsparing sustenance, and for the glorious intellectual partnership and life that we share. I dedicate this book to him.

Notes

1. Illumination

1. Louis Barron, *Sous le drapeau rouge* (Paris: A. Savine, 1889), 117, 111.

2. Barron, *Sous le drapeau*, 117, 113.

3. Maxime Vuillaume, *Mes cahiers rouge au temps de la Commune* (Paris: P. Ollendorff, 1909), 281–283.

4. John Merriman, *Massacre: The Life and Death of the Paris Commune* (New York: Basic Books, 2014), 132.

5. Louise Michel, *La Commune: Histoire et souvenirs* (1898; Paris: La Découverte, 1970), 242.

6. Eugène Hennebert, *Guerre des communeux de Paris: 18 mars–28 mai 1871/ par un officier supérieur de l'armée de Versailles* (Paris: Fermin Didot Frères, 1871), 119.

7. Michel, *La Commune*, 242.

8. While the word "feminist" did not come into use until the 1890s, people have long fought against gender inequities, and using the contemporary term appropriately labels these activists.

9. *London Standard*, June 1871.

10. Frank Jellinek, *The Paris Commune of 1871* (1937; New York: Universal Library, 1965), 42.

11. Jellinek, *Paris Commune*, 42.

12. André Léo, Elisée Reclus, and Paul Lacombe, in *L'Agriculteur* (Paris, 1869).

13. *Code Civil de France* (Paris: L'Imprimerie de la République, 1804).

14. It also advanced equal access to work for women and secular primary education for girls (the Catholic Church controlled girls' education in this period).

15. André Léo, "Manifesto," *L'Opinion Nationale*, July 7, 1868.

16. Alain Dalotel, Alain Faure, and Jean-Claude Freiermuth, *Aux origines de la Commune: Le movement des reunions publiques à Paris 1868–1870* (Paris: Maspero, 1980), 149.

17. André Léo, *L'Opinion nationale*, July 18, 1868.

18. Dalotel et al., *Aux origines*, 157, 153.

19. Dalotel et al., *Aux origines*, 202, 171.

20. Dalotel et al., *Aux origines*, 204.

21. Dalotel et al., *Aux origines*, 248.

22. Dalotel et al., *Aux origines*, 218.

23. Dalotel et al., *Aux origines*, 169. We do not know the first names of either of these women.

24. Dalotel et al., *Aux origines*, 123–126.

25. Eugène Varlin, *Pratique militante et ecris d'un ouvrier communard*, edited by Paule Lejeune (Paris: Maspero, 1971); Jacques Rougerie, *Eugène Varlin: Aux origines du mouvement ouvrier* (Paris: Editions du Détour, 2020).

26. P.-J. Proudhon, "De la Justice dans la Révolution et dans l'Eglise," in *Women, the Family, and Freedom: The Debate in Documents*, edited by Karen Offen and Susan Groag Bell (Stanford, CA: Stanford University Press, 1983), 330.

27. Varlin, *Pratique militante*, 35, 31.

28. Varlin, *Pratique militante*, 25.

29. This, of course, remains an unattained goal across the globe to this day.

30. Cecelia Beach, "Bibliographie de André Léo," in *Les vies d'André Léo: Romancière, féministe et communarde*, edited by Frédéric Chauvaud et al. (Rennes: Presses Universitaires de Rennes, 2015), 311–333.

31. Stewart Edwards, *The Paris Commune 1871* (New York: Quadrangle Books, 1971), 36.

32. Michel, *La Commune*, 38.

33. Michel, *La Commune*, 38.

34. "Les Grèves," *Le Temps* (Paris), June 8, 1870.

35. In Dalotel et al., *Aux origines*, 268.

36. In Dalotel et al., *Aux origines*, 269.

37. Charles Sutter-Laumann, *Histoire d'un trente sous, 1870–1871* (Paris: Albert Savine, 1891), 35, 38.

38. Gèrard Noiriel, *Une histoire populaire de la France: De la guerre de Cent Ans à nos jours* (Marseilles: Agone, 2018), 368.

39. André Léo, "Le Quatre septembre," La Siège, *Mémoires*, Descaves Collection, IISH.

40. Michel, *La Commune*, 19.

41. Léo, "Le Quartre septembre."

42. Joseph Comte D'Haussonville, *Mon journal pendant la guerre (1870–1871)* (Paris: Calmann-Levy, 1905), 110–111.

43. Edwards, *The Paris Commune*, 45–46.

44. Francisque Sarcey, *Le siège de Paris: Impressions et souvenirs* (Paris: E. Lachaud, 1871), 87.

45. Maxime Vuillaume, "Le Rétour de Victor Hugo," *Le Matin* (Paris), September 12, 1912.

46. *Le Rappel* (Paris), September 7, 1870.

47. Capitalization in the original. *Le Rappel* (Paris), September 4, 1870.

48. *Le Rappel* (Paris), September 9, 1870.

49. Sarcey, *Le siège de Paris*, 167–168.

50. Hollis Clayson, *Paris in Despair: Art and Everyday Life under Siege (1870–1871)* (Chicago: University of Chicago Press, 2002), 173–174.

51. Clayson, *Paris in Despair*, 174–175; Menu, Restaurant Voisin, December 25, 1870.

52. Sarcey, *Le siège de Paris*, 171.

53. Eugène Kerbaul, *Nathalie Le Mel: Une Bretonne révolutionnaire et féministe* (Paris: Chez l'auteur, 1997), 41.

54. "Société démocratique de moralisation par le travail," LY7, Service Historique de la Défense (SHD).

55. "Aux femmes de Paris," *La Patrie en danger*, September 13, 1870.

56. André Léo, "La Marseillaise des femmes," *La Petite Presse* (Paris), September 10, 1870.

57. Georges Duveau, *Le siège de Paris: Septembre 1870–janvier 1871* (Paris: Hachette, 1939), 182.

58. Merriman, *Massacre*, 12–15.

59. Merriman, *Massacre*, 12–15.; Dalotel et al., *Aux origines*, 255–256.

60. Michel, *La Commune*, 101–102.

61. Paule Mink, "Les Canons du 18 mars," *La Petite république* (Paris), March 18, 1895.

62. Varlin, *Pratique militante*, 150.

63. Michel, *La Commune*, 112.

64. André Léo, "La Provence," *Mémoires*, 14, Descaves Collection, IISH.

65. Michel, *La Commune*, 113.

66. Léo, "La Provence," *Mémoires*, 14, Descaves Collection, IISH.

67. Adolphe Thiers, "Habitants de Paris," March 17, 1871. http://archives .paris.fr/a/850/adresse-d-adolphe-thiers-aux-habitant-e-s-de-paris-au -sujet-de-la-reprise-des-canons-de-la-garde-nationale/.

68. Hennebert, *Guerre des communeaux*, 68.

69. Michel, *La Commune*, 129–130.

70. Sutter-Laumann, *Histoire d'un trente sous*, 225.

71. Anonymous, *La vérité sur la Commune*, 232, in Gay Gullickson, *Unruly Women of Paris* (Ithaca, NY: Cornell University Press, 1996), 28–29.

72. Merriman, *Massacre*, 29.

73. Michel, *La Commune*, 130.

2. Fluorescence

1. Victorine Brocher, *Souvenirs d'une morte vivante* (1909; Paris: La Découverte, 2002), 156–157.

2. Emile Duval à Marie Huot, "Ma chère femme," in *Émile Duval (1840–1871), général de la Commune*, by Pierre-Henri Zaidman (Paris: Editions Dittmar, 2006), 190n2.

3. "Aux Peuple," Le Comité Central de la Guard National, March 19, 1871.

4. "Citoyens," Le Comité Central de la Guard National, March 19, 1871.

5. Louise Michel, *La Commune: Histoire et souvenirs* (1898; Paris: La Découverte, 1970), 131–132.

6. Louise Michel, *Mémoires* (1886; Paris: Sulliver, 1998), 115.

7. Adolphe Thiers, March 19, 1871, in Michel, *La Commune*, 135.

8. Quoted in Zaidman, *Émile Duval*, 192.

9. Quoted in Stewart Edwards, *The Paris Commune 1871* (New York: Quadrangle Books, 1971), 161.

10. "The Revolution in Paris," *Chicago Tribune*, March 21, 1871.

11. "Déclaration des maires et des députés de Paris, réunis en conseil à Saint-Germain-l'auxerrois le 25 mars 1871," in Michel, *La Commune,* 141–142.

12. Adolphe Thiers, March 25, 1871, in Michel, *La Commune, 142.*

13. Élie Reclus, *La Commune de Paris au jour le jour* (Paris: Schleicher Frères, 1908), 40.

14. *Le Cri du people,* May 28, 1871.

15. La Commune de Paris, May 28, 1871, in Michel, *La Commune,* 148–151.

16. "Declaration au peuple français," *Journal Officiel,* April 20, 1871; Massimiliano Tomba, *Insurgent Universality: An Alternative Legacy of Modernity* (New York: Oxford University Press, 2019), 89–98.

17. Martin Johnson, *The Paradise of Association: Political Culture and Popular Organizations in the Paris Commune of 1871* (Ann Arbor: University of Michigan Press, 1996).

18. Benoît Malon, *La troisième défaite du prolétariat français* (Neuchâtel: Guillaume Fils, 1871), 270.

19. Prosper-Olivier Lissagaray, *Histoire de la Commune de 1871* (Paris: Dentu, 1896), 306.

20. Marforio (pseud. Louise Lacroix), *Les Écharpes rouges: Souvenirs de la Commune* (Paris: A. Laporte, 1872), 20–21.

21. Paul Fontoulieu, *Les Églises de Paris sous la Commune* (Paris. E. Dentu, 1873), 63–64; https://maitron.fr/spip.php?article69999, notice ROGISSART Marie, Catherine, in *Le Maitron Dictionnaire biographique,* version mise en ligne le 26 juillet 2009, dernière modification le 30 juin 2020.

22. Marforio, *Les Écharpes rouges,* 20–21.

23. Fontoulieu, *Les Églises,* 64.

24. Fontoulieu, *Les Églises,* 216.

25. Fontoulieu, *Les Églises,* 216.

26. Fontoulieu, *Les Églises,* 288.

27. Marforio, *Les Écharpes,* 155.

28. Fontoulieu, *Les Églises,* 254.

29. Tomba, *Insurgent Universality,* 96–98.

30. John Merriman, *Massacre: The Life and Death of the Paris Commune* (New York: Basic Books, 2014), 39–41.

31. Adolphe Thiers, *Histoire de la révolution du 4 septembre [1870] et de l'insurrection du 18 mars [1871]* (Paris: Garnier Frères, 1873), 136–143.

32. Merriman, *Massacre*, 34.

33. André Léo, "Signes, précurseurs," *Mémoires*, 15, Descaves Collection, IISH.

34. Fontoulieu, *Les Églises*, 62.

35. Fontoulieu, *Les Églises*, 62.

36. Edmond de Goncourt and Jules de Goncourt, *Journal de Goncourt: Mémoires de la vie litteraire*, vol. 4 (Paris: Bibliothèque-Charpentier, 1890), 230.

37. Eugène Varlin, *Pratique militante et ecris d'un ouvrier communard*, edited by Paule Lejeune (Paris: Maspero, 1971), 158–160.

38. Quoted in Jacques Rougerie, *Eugène Varlin: Aux origines du mouvement ouvrier* (Paris: Editions du Detour, 2019), 167.

39. Eric Cavaterra, *La Banque de France et la Commune de Paris (1871)* (Paris: L'Harmattan, 1998).

40. *Journal Officiel*, April 26, 1871, 379–390.

41. *Journal Officiel*, April 26, 1871, 379–390.

42. Pierre-Joseph Proudhon, *Qu'est-ce que la propriété?* (Paris: Prévot, 1841).

43. *Journal Officiel*, April 17, 1871.

44. *Journal Officiel*, April 17, 1871.

45. Elisabeth Dmitrieff, "Appel aux citoyennes de Paris," *Journal Officiel*, April 11, 1871.

46. Membres des Comités, Union des femmes, LY23, SHD.

47. "Adresse des citoyennes," *Journal Officiel*, April 14, 1871.

48. Quoted in Edwards, *The Paris Commune*, 257; *Procès-Verbaux de la Commune de Paris*, April 28, 1871.

49. *Procès-Verbaux de la Commune de Paris*, April 28, 1871.

50. "Adresse du Comité Central de l'Union des femmes à la Commission de travail et d'échange," Union des femmes, LY 22, SHD.

51. "Adresse du Comité Central de l'Union des femmes à la Commission de travail et d'échange," Union des femmes, LY 22, SHD.

52. *Journal Officiel*, May 16, 1871.

53. Quoted in Charles-Jérôme Lecour, *La Prostitution à Paris et à Londres (1789–1871)* (Paris: P. Asselin, 1877), 324–325.

54. Louise Michel, *Mémoires de Louise Michel écrits par elle-même* (Paris: F. Roy, 1886), 363.

55. In Lecour, *La Prostitution*, 323. The declaration was signed by Eugène Pottier, Auguste Serallier, Jacques Durand, and Jules-Paul Johannard.

56. Louise Michel, *Souvenirs et aventures de ma vie* (Paris: La Découverte/ Maspero, 1983), 26–27.

57. Michel, *Souvenirs et aventures de ma vie*, 27.

58. *Journal Officiel*, April 6, 1871.

59. Kristin Ross, *Communal Luxury: The Political Imaginary of the Paris Commune* (New York: Verso, 2015), 50.

60. *Journal Officiel*, April 15, 1871.

61. Ross, *Communal Luxury*, 52–57.

62. Gonzalo Sanchez, *Organizing Independence: The Artists Federation of the Paris Commune and Its Legacy, 1871–1889* (Lincoln: University of Nebraska Press, 1997).

63. Ross, *Communal Luxury*, 44–65.

64. *Le Vengeur*, April 8, 1871.

65. Marie Galvez, "La bibliothèque national et la Commune de Paris (18 mars–28 mai, 1871)," *Revue de la BnF* 2, no. 50 (2015): 70–85.

66. Paul Reclus, *Les Frères Élie et Élisée Reclus* (Paris: Les Amis d'Élisée Reclus, 1964), 181–182.

67. Galvez, "La bibliothèque nationale," 70–85.

68. Quoted in Galvez, "La bibliothèque nationale," 81.

69. Quoted in Galvez, "La bibliothèque nationale," 83. *Journal des journaux de la Commune*, vol. 2 (Paris: Garnier Frères, 1872), 561.

70. Michel, *La Commune*, 156.

71. Gustave Courbet à ses parents, April 30, 1871, in Michèle Riot-Sarcey, *Le procès de la liberté: Une histoire souterraine du XIXe siècle en France* (Paris: La Découverte, 2016), 250.

72. Quoted in Persis Hunt, "Feminism and Anti-Clericalism under the Commune," *Massachusetts Review* 12 (Summer 1971), 419.

73. Quoted in Hunt, "Feminism and Anti-Clericalism," 420.

74. Serge Wolikow, "Les Instituteurs et la Commune," *La Nouvelle critique* (February 1971), 81–94.

75. André Léo, *Le Siècle* (Paris), July 16, 1870. Many of Léo's novels, published between 1865 and her death in 1900, addressed ideas of free and republican education. Cecilia Beach, "*Savoir c'est pouvoir:* Integral Education in the Novels of André Léo," *Nineteenth Century French Studies* 36, nos. 3–4 (Spring–Summer 2008): 270–285.

76. *Le Vengeur*, April 8, 1871.

77. Jean-Francois Dupeyron, *À l'école de la Commune de Paris. L'histoire d'une autre école* (Dijon: Editions Raison et Passions, 2020), 161.

78. *Journal Officiel*, April 2, 1871.

79. Dupeyron, *À l'école de la Commune*, 99–100.

80. *Journal Officiel*, May 17, 1871.

81. "Maison des orphelins de la Commune de Paris, Mairie du 3e arrondissement," in *Les Murailles politiques françaises*, vol. 2: *La Commune* (Paris: Le Chavalier, 1874), 520.

82. "Maison des orphelins de la Commune de Paris."

83. In Dupeyron, *A l'école de la Commune*, 100.

84. Dupeyron, *A l'école de la Commune*, 105–106.

85. *Journal Officiel*, April 2, 1871.

86. *Le Réveil du people*, April 23, 1871.

87. *Journal Officiel*, May 15, 1871.

88. *Le Vengeur*, April 3, 1871, in Claudine Rey, Annie Gayat, and Sylvie Pepino, *Petit dictionnaire des femmes de la Commune: Les oubliées de l'histoire* (Paris: Editions Le bruit des autres, 2013), 103–104.

89. *Journal Officiel*, May 13, 1871.

90. *Journal Officiel*, April 13, 1871.

91. Maxime Jourdan, *Le Cri du peuple (22 février 1871–23 mai 1871)* (Paris: L'Harmattan, 2005), 13.

92. *Le Drapeau rouge*, n.d.; *Le Fédéraliste*, May 1871; *L'Ouvrier de l'avenir*, March 1871; *L'Ordre*, March 1871; *Le Prolétaire*, May 15, 1871.

93. *Le Prolétaire*, May 10, 1871.

94. *Père Duchêne*, March 21, 1871.

95. *Père Duchêne*, March 16, 1871.

96. *Le Cri du peuple*, April 21, 1871.

97. André Léo, *La Sociale*, April 22, 1871.

98. "La Révolution sans la femme," *La Sociale*, May 8, 1871.

99. Michel, *La Commune*, 193.

100. André Léo, "Toutes avec tous," *La Sociale*, April 12, 1871.

101. André Léo, "Aventures de neuf ambulancières," *La Sociale*, May 6, 1871.

102. Auguste Villiers de L'Isle-Adam, cited and translated in Edwards, *The Communards of Paris, 1871* (Ithaca, NY: Cornell University Press, 1973), 142.

103. Laure Godineau, *La Commune de Paris par ceux qui l'ont vécu* (Paris: Parigramme, 2010), 111–114.

104. Wilhelm Dineson, *Paris under Communen, Paris sous la Commune* (Paris: Michel de Maule, 2003).

3. Explosion

1. *Journal Officiel*, May 24, 1871.

2. Élie Reclus, *La Commune de Paris au jour le jour* (Paris: Schleicher Frères, 1908), 304.

3. John Merriman, *Massacre: The Life and Death of the Paris Commune* (New York: Basic Books, 2014), 204–209.

4. *Journal Officiel*, May 22, 1871.

5. Merriman, *Massacre*, 144.

6. Louise Michel, *Memoires de Louise Michel écrits par elle-même* (Paris: F. Roy, 1886), 126.

7. Béatrix Excoffon, "Récit de Béatrix Excoffon," in Louise Michel, *La Commune: Histoire et souvenirs* (1898; Paris: La Découverte, 1970), 353–354.

8. W. Pembroke Fetridge, *The Rise and Fall of the Paris Commune, with a Full Account of the Bombardment, Capture, and Burning of the City* (New York: Harper & Bros., 1871), 287–288.

9. Fetridge, *The Rise and Fall*, 291.

10. Fetridge, *The Rise and Fall*, 291–292.

11. Jean-Claude Farcy, "Une source inédite: Le registre des enfants de la Commune de Paris (1871)," *Criminocorpus* (September 2020), http://journals.openedition.org/criminocorpus/7417.

12. Quentin Deluermoz, "Les gamins de Paris au combat? Les enfants-soldats sous la Commune de Paris (1871)" (paper presented at L'enfant-combattant, pratiques et réprésentations, Amiens, France, November 2010), http://www.enfance-violence-exil.net/index.php/ecms/it/3/344.

13. Frank Jellinek, *The Paris Commune of 1871* (1937; New York: Universal Library, 1965), 326–326; Merriman, *Massacre*, 156.

14. In Jellinek, *The Paris Commune*, 327.

15. Jellinek, *The Paris Commune*, 326–327; Merriman, *Massacre*, 156.

16. "Manifeste du Comité Central de l'Union des femmes pour la défense de Paris et les soins aux blessés," May 6, 1871, LY 22, 23, SHD.

17. In Sylvie Braibant, *Elisabeth Dmitrieff aristocrate et pétroleuse* (Paris: Belfond, 1993), 156.

18. Merriman, *Massacre*, 112–113.

19. Quentin Deluermoz, *Commune(s) 1870–1871: Une traverse des mondes au xix siècle* (Paris: Editions du Seuil, 2020), 235–238; Eric Fournier, *Paris en ruines* (Paris: Editions Imago, 2008).

20. Stewart Edwards, ed., *The Paris Commune 1871* (New York: Quadrangle Books, 1971), 323–327.

21. Edwards, *The Paris Commune*, 326–327.

22. Benoît Malon, *La troisième défaite du prolétariat français* (Neuchâtel: Guillaume Fils, 1871), 432.

23. Augustine-Malvina Blanchecotte, *Tablettes d'une femme pendant la Commune* (Paris: Didier et Cie., 1872), 260.

24. Louis Gallet, *Guerre et Commune, impressions d'un hospitalier. 1870–1871* (Paris: C. Levy, 1998), 225.

25. Edwards, *The Paris Commune*, 327–328.

26. In Gay Gullickson, *Unruly Women of Paris: Images of the Commune* (Ithaca, NY: Cornell University Press, 1996), 172.

27. Eugène Hennebert, *Guerre des commueaux de Paris: 18 mars–28 mai 1871/ par un officier supérieur de l'armée de Versailles* (Paris: Fermin Didot Frères, 1871), 237.

28. Maxime du Camp, *Les Convulsions de Paris* (Paris: Librairie Hachette, 1880), 286.

29. Among the hundreds of books written on the Commune, Thomas's was the first to recognize the centrality of women to the revolution.

30. Edith Thomas, *Les Pétroleuses* (Paris: Gallimard, 1963), 189–209.

31. See, among others, Michèle Audin, *La Semaine sanglante: Mai 1871, légendes et comptes* (Paris: Libertalia, 1871); Alain Dalotel, "La barricade des femmes," in *La Barricade*, edited by Alain Corbin and Jean-Marie Mayeur (Paris: Editions de la Sorbonne, 1997).

32. *Journal Officiel*, May 24, 1871.

33. Michèle Audin, "La 'barricade tenue par des femmes,' une légende?" https://macommunedeparis.com/2017/07/10/la-barricade-tenue-par-des -femmes-une-legende/; Charles Sutter-Laumann, *Histoire d'un trente sous, 1870–1871* (Paris: Albert Savine, 1891), 304; Michel, La *Commune*, 233.

34. Briot à Ministre de la guerre, LY 7, SHD.

35. Briot à Ministre de la guerre.

36. Maxime du Camp, *Les Convulsions de Paris* (Paris: Librairie Hachette, 1880), 60–61.

37. Emile Zola, *Le Sémaphore de Marseille*, May 18–19, 1871.

38. Michel, *La Commune*, 236.

39. *New York Times*, May 25, 1871.

40. Edwards, *The Paris Commune*, 330–331.

41. Geneviève Breton, *Journal, 1867–1871* (Paris: Ramsay, 1985), 241.

42. Sutter-Laumann, *Histoire d'un trente sous*, 335

43. Blanchecotte, *Tablettes d'une femme*, 279.

44. Jean-Baptiste Clément, *La Revanche des communeux: 1871*, vol. 1, 2nd ed. (Paris: J. Marie, 1887–1887), 10.

45. Maxime Vuillaume, *Mes Cahiers rouge au temps de la Commune* (Paris: P. Ollendorff, 1909).

46. Italics in original. Prosper-Olivier Lissagaray, *Huit journées en mai derrières les barricades* (Brussels: Bureau du petit journal, 1871), 170–171.

47. Jules Bergeret, *Le dix-huit mars: Journal hebdomodaire*, in Gay Gullickson, *Unruly Women of Paris* (Ithaca, NY: Cornell University Press, 1996), 180.

48. Georges Jenneret, *Paris pendant la Commune révolutionnaire de 71* (Neuchâtel: n.p., 1871), 250.

49. In Gaston de Costa, *La Commune vécu: 18 mars–28 mai 1871* (Paris: Ancienne Maison Quantin, 1903), 436–441.

50. Michèle Audin is the first Commune scholar to recognize Versailles troops' use of rape as a tool of gendered repression and reprisal, contesting Robert Tombs's unsupported contentions that such sexual violence was "unlikely" and "virtually non-existent." Audin, "Les viols," in *La Semaine sanglante*.

51. Laure Godineau, *La Commune de Paris par ceux qui l'ont vécu* (Paris: Parigramme, 2010), 218–220; Merriman, *Massacre*, 187–188.

52. Camille Pelletan, *La Semaine de mai* (Paris: Maurice Dreyfous, 1880), 335–339.

53. Pelletan, *La Semaine de mai*, 335–339.

54. Adolphe Thiers, May 25, 1871, in Alfred Dubreuil Hélion de La Gueronnière, *Histoire de la guerre de 1870–71: L'invasion, les désastres, la Commune* (Charleville: Colle-Louis, 1871), 822.

55. Sutter-Laumann, *Histoire d'un trente sous*, 335–336.

56. Sutter-Laumann, *Histoire d'un trente sous*, 335–336.

57. Reclus, *La Commune de Paris*, xii, 353.

58. Paul Fontoulieu, *Les Églises de Paris sous la Commune* (Paris: E. Dentu, 1873), 81–82; Merriman, *Massacre*, 87–88, 122–123, 180–184.

59. Godineau, *La Commune de Paris*, 210–212.

60. Victor Hugo, *L'Année Terrible* (Paris: Michel Lévy, 1872), 215.

61. Jacques Rougèrie, *Eugène Varlin: Aux origins du movement ouvrier* (Paris: Editions du Détour, 2020), 186–190; Malon, *La troisième défaite*, 479; Eugène Varlin, *Pratique militante et écris d'un ouvrier communard*, edited by Paule Lejeune (Paris: Maspero, 1971), 186–187.

62. Jules Vallès, *La Liberté* (Belgium), June 4, 1871, in Rougérie, *Eugène Varlin*, 189–190.

63. Rapport sur l'affaire Dmitrieff, May 23, 1872, LY22, SHD.

64. Michel, *Mémoires*, 430–432.

65. Michel, *Mémoires*, 198–199.

66. Michel, *La Commune*, 256–61.

67. *New York Daily News*, May 26, 1871.

68. Récit de Béatrix Excoffons, in Michel, *La Commune*, 353–354.

69. Prosper-Olivier Lissagaray, *Histoire de la Commune de 1871* (Paris: Maspero, 1970), 386–387.

70. Gullickson, *Unruly Women*, 192.

71. Procès de Louise Michel, 6e Conseil de guerre, in Michel, *La Commune*, 327–337.

72. They also deported a much smaller number to the older penal colony in French Guyana.

73. *Enquêtes parlementaires sur l'insurrection du 18 mars* (Paris: Librarie Germer-Baillière, 1872), 3, 247.

74. Alice Bullard, *Exile to Paradise* (Stanford, CA: Stanford University Press, 2000), 87–97.

75. Quentin Deluermoz, *Commune(s) 1870–1871: Une traverse des mondes au xix siècle* (Paris: Editions du Seuil, 2020), 259–266.

76. Théophile Gautier, *Tableaux de siège: Paris, 1870–1871* (Paris: Charpentier, 1871), 372–373.

77. Blanchecotte, *Tablettes d'une femme*, 308.

78. Jellinek, *The Paris Commune*, 370.

79. Robert Tombs, "How Bloody Was *La Semaine Sanglante*? A Revision," *Historical Journal* 55, no. 3 (2012): 679–704.

80. See, most recently, historian and mathematician Michèle Audin's meticulous analysis in *La Semaine sanglante*.

81. "Quoi! d'un côté la France et de l'autre la France! Arrêtez! c'est le deuil qui sort de vos succès." Victor Hugo, *L'Année terrible* (Paris: Michel Lévy, 1872), 175.

82. Deluermoz, *Commune(s)*, 67–74.

83. Jacqueline Couti, "Firestarters: Insurgent Women in the Insurrection of Southern Martinique and the Paris Commune," *The Funambulist: Politics of Space and Bodies* 34 (March–April 2021): 16–19.

84. The Algerian colonist Communards did not support the Indigenous Kabyle in their anti-imperial revolt. Niklas Plaetzer, "Decolonizing the 'Universal Republic': The Paris Commune and French Empire," *Nineteenth-Century French Studies* 49, nos. 3–4 (Spring–Summer 2021): 585–603; Deluermoz, *Commune(s)*, 67–74.

85. Lucy E. Parsons, *Life of Albert R. Parsons, with a Brief History of the Labor Movement in America* (1903), xxvii, Northern Illinois University Digital Collections, DeKalb, IL, https://digital.lib.niu.edu/islandora/object/niu-gildedage%3A24434.

86. Deluermoz, *Commune(s)*, 312–315; J. Michelle Coghlan, *Sensational Internationalism: The Paris Commune and the Remapping of American Memory in the Long Nineteenth Century* (Edinburgh: Edinburgh University Press, 2016), 130; Anthony Gorman, "Internationalist Thought, Local Practice: Life and Death in the Anarchist Movement in 1890s Egypt," in *The Long 1890s in Egypt: Colonial Quiescence, Subterranean Resistance,* edited by Marilyn Booth and Tony Gorman (Edinburgh: Edinburgh University Press, 2014), 229.

Bibliography

Archives

Archives de la Préfecture de la Police (APP), Paris.
Archives Nationales (France) (AN), Paris.
Bibliothèque Historique de la Ville de Paris (BHVP), Paris.
Bibliothèque Marguerite Durand (BMD), Paris.
Bibliothèque Nationale (BN), Paris.
Eugene W. Schulkind Paris Commune Archive (ESPCA), University of
  Sussex.
International Institute of Social History (IISH), Amsterdam.
Service Historique de la Défense (SHD), Vincennes, Paris.

Primary Sources

L'Agriculteur. Paris, 1870.
Arnault, Louis. *Le Socialisme et la Commune: Insurrection du 18 mars 1871.*
  Paris: Alphonse Picard, 1875.
Arnould, Arthur. *Historie Populaire et parlementaire de la Commune de Paris.*
  Lyon: Editions Jacques-Maris Laffont, 1871.
Barron, Louis. *Sous le drapeau rouge.* Paris: A. Savine, 1889.
Blanchecotte, Augustine-Malvina. *Tablettes d'une femme pendant la
  Commune.* Paris: Didier et Cie., 1872.
Breton, Geneviève. *Journal, 1867–1871.* Paris: Ramsay, 1985.
Brocher, Victorine. *Souvenirs d'une morte vivante.* Paris: La Découverte,
  2002. (First published 1909 by A. Lapie.)
Camp, Maxime du. *Les Convulsions de Paris.* Paris: Librairie Hachette, 1880.

Chicago Tribune. March 1871.

Clément, Jean-Baptiste. *La Revanche des communeux: 1871,* vol. 1, 2nd ed. Paris: J. Marie, 1887–1887.

Code Civil de France. Paris: L'Imprimerie de la République, 1804.

La Commune. Paris, March–May 1871.

Commission ouvrière de 1867: Recueil des procès-verbaux. Edited by Eugène Tataret. Paris: Imprimerie Augros, 1868.

Le Cri du peuple. February–May 1871.

da Costa, Gaston. *La Commune vécu: 18 mars–28 mai 1871.* Paris: Ancienne Maison Quantin, 1903.

Delmas, l'Abbé. *La Terreur et l'église en 1871.* Paris: E. Dentu, 1871.

Descaves Collection, IISH.

Le Drapeau Rouge. Paris, n.d.

L'Egalité. Paris, March–May 1871.

Enquêtes parlementaires sur l'insurrection du 18 mars. Paris: Librarie Germer-Ballière, 1872.

Excoffon, Béatrix. "Récit de Béatrix Excofon." In *La Commune: Histoire et souvenirs,* by Louise Michel. Paris: La Découverte, 1970. (First published 1898 by P. V. Stock.)

Le Fédéraliste. Paris, May, 1871.

Fetridge, W. Pembroke. *The Rise and Fall of the Paris Commune, with a Full Account of the Bombardment, Capture, and Burning of the City.* New York: Harper & Bros., 1871.

Fonds Marie-Louise Bouglé, BHVP.

Fontoulieu, Paul. *Les Églises de Paris sous la Commune.* Paris: E. Dentu, 1873.

Gallet, Louis. *Guerre et Commune, impressions d'un hospitalier, 1870–1871.* Paris: C. Levy, 1898.

Gautier, Théophile. *Tableaux de siège: Paris, 1870–1871.* Paris: Charpentier, 1871.

de Goncourt, Edmond, and Jules de Goncourt. *Journal de Goncourt: Mémoires de la vie litteraire,* vol. 4. Paris: Bibliothèque-Charpentier, 1890.

Guénin, L.-P. *Massacre de la rue Haxo.* Paris: Librarie de "l'Echo de la Sorbonne," 1872.

Guillaume, James. *L'Internationale: Documents et souvenirs (1864–1878).* 2 vols. Paris: Société Nouvelle de Librairie et d'Edition, 1905.

D'Haussonville, Joseph Comte. *Mon journal pendant la guerre (1870–1871)*. Paris: Calmann-Levy, 1905.

Hennebert, Eugène. *Guerre des communeux de Paris: 18 mars–28 mai 1871/ par un officier supérieur de l'armée de Versailles.* Paris: Fermin Didot Frères, 1871.

Hugo, Victor. *L'Année terrible.* Paris: Michel Lévy, 1872.

Jeanneret, Georges. *Paris pendant la Commune révolutionnaire de 71.* Neuchâtel: n.p., 1871.

Journal des journaux de la Commune, vol. 2. Paris: Garnier Frères, 1872.

Journal Officiel (Commune). Paris, April–May 1871.

de La Gueronnière, Alfred Dubreuil Hélion. *Histoire de la guerre de 1870–71: l'Invasion, les désastres, la Commune.* Charleville: Colle-Louis, 1871.

Lecour, Charles-Jérome. *La Prostitution à Paris et à Londres (1789–1871).* Paris: P. Asselin, 1877.

Léo, André [Léodile Béra Champseix]. *La Guerre sociale.* Paris: Le passager clandestin, 2011. (First published 1871 by Guillaume et fils.)

Lissagaray, Prosper-Olivier. *Histoire de la Commune de 1871.* Paris: Dentu, 1896.

———. *Les Huit journées en mai derrière les barricades.* Brussels: Bureau du petit journal, 1871.

London Standard. June 1871.

Malon, Benoît. *La Troisième défaite du prolétariat français.* Neuchâtel: Guillaume Fils, 1871.

Marforio [Louise Lacroix]. *Les Écharpes rouges: Souvenirs de la Commune.* Paris: A. Laporte, 1872.

Le Matin. Paris, September 1912.

Marx, Karl, and V. I. Lenin. *Civil War in France: The Paris Commune.* New York: International Publishers, 1940.

Michel, Louise. *La Commune: Histoire et souvenirs.* Paris: La Découverte, 1970. (First published 1898 by P. V. Stock.)

———. *Je vous écris de ma nuit: Correspondance générale, 1850–1904.* Edited by Xavière Gauthier. Paris: Les Editions de Paris, 1999.

———. *Mémoires de Louise Michel écrits par elle-même.* Paris: F. Roy, 1886.

———. *Souvenirs et aventures de ma vie.* Paris: La Découverte/Maspero. 1983.

Mink, Paule. *Paule Mink: Communarde et féministe 1839–1901.* Edited by
    Alain Dalotel. Paris: Syros, 1981.

Les Murailles politiques françaises, vol. 2: *La Commune.* Paris: Le Chevalier,
    1874.

Molinari, M. G. *Les Clubs rouge pendant le siège de Paris.* Paris: Garnier
    Frères, 1871.

Murailles politiques français. 2 vols. Paris: L. Le Chevalier, 1874.

New York Daily News. May 1871.

New York Times. May 1871.

L'Opinion Nationale. Paris, July–September 1868.

L'Ouvrier de l'avenir. March, 1871.

L'Ordre. March, 1871.

Parsons, Lucy E. *Life of Albert R. Parsons, with a Brief History of the Labor
    Movement in America* (1903). Northern Illinois University Digital
    Collections, DeKalb, IL. https://digital.lib.niu.edu/islandora/object
    /niu-gildedage%3A24434.

La Patrie en danger. Paris, September 1870.

Pelletan, Camille. *La Semaine de mai.* Paris: Maurice Dreyfous, 1880.

Le Père Duchêne. Paris, March 1871.

La Petite Presse. Paris, September 1870.

La Petite république. Paris, March 1895.

Procès-Verbaux de la Commune de Paris. April 1871.

Le Prolétaire. Paris, May 1871.

Proudhon, P.-J. "De la Justice dans la Révolution et dans l'Eglise." In
    Women, the Family, and Freedom: The Debate in Documents, edited by
    Karen Offen and Susan Groag Bell, 330. Stanford, CA: Stanford
    University Press, 1983.

Proudhon, Pierre-Joseph. *Qu'est-ce que la propriété?* Paris: Prévot, 1841.

Le Rappel. Paris, September 1870.

Reclus, Élie. *La Commune de Paris au jour le jour.* Paris: Schleicher Frères,
    1908.

Reclus, Paul. *Les Frères Élie et Élisée Reclus.* Paris: Les Amis d'Élisée
    Reclus, 1964.

Le Réveil du peuple. Paris, March–May 1871.

Sarcey, Francisque. *Le Siège de Paris: Impressions et souvenirs.* Paris:
    E. Lachaud, 1871.

Le Sémaphore de Marseille. May 1871.

Le Siècle. Paris, July 1870.

La Sociale. Paris, March–May 1871.

Sutter-Laumann, Charles. *Histoire d'un trente sous, 1870–1871.* Paris: Albert
Savine, 1891.

Le Temps. Paris, June 1870.

Thiers, Adolphe. *Histoire de la révolution du 4 septembre [1870] et de
l'insurrection du 18 mars [1871].* Paris: Garnier Frères, 1873.

Le Vengeur. Paris, April 1871.

Vuillaume, Maxime. *Mes cahiers rouge au temps de la Commune.* Paris:
P. Ollendorff, 1909.

Secondary Sources

Archer, Julian P. W. *The First International in France (1864–1872): Its
Origins, Theories and Impact.* New York: Lanham, 1997.

Audin, Michèle. *La Commune de Paris.* https://macommunedeparis.com/.

———. *La Semaine sanglante: Mai 1871, légendes et comptes.* Paris: Editions
Libertalia, 1871.

Boime, Alfred. *Art and the French Commune: Imagining Paris after War and
Revolution.* Princeton, NJ: Princeton University Press, 1994.

Boxer, Marilyn. "Socialism Faces Feminism in France: 1879–1913." PhD
dissertation, University of California, Riverside, 1975.

Braibant, Sylvie. *Elisabeth Dmitrieff, aristocrate et pétroleuse.* Paris: Belfond,
1993.

Bruhat, Jean, Jean Dautry, and Emile Tersen. *La Commune de 1871.* Paris:
Editions Sociales, 1970.

Bullard, Alice. *Exile to Paradise: Savagery and Civilization in Paris and the
South Pacific, 1790–1900.* Stanford, CA: Stanford University Press, 2000.

Cavaterra, Éric. *La Banque de France et la Commune de Paris (1871).* Paris:
L'Harmattan, 1998.

César, Marc, and Laure Godineau, eds. *La Commune de 1871: Une relecture.*
Grâne: Editions Créaphis, 2019.

Chang, Domenica. "'Un Nouveau '93': Discourses of Mimicry and Terror
in the Paris Commune of 1871." *French Historical Studies* 36, no. 4 (Fall
2013): 629–648.

Chauvaud, Frédéric, François Dubasque, Pierre Rossignol, and Louis Vibrac, eds. *Les Vies d'André Léo: Romancière, féministe, et communarde.* Rennes: Presses Universitaires de Rennes, 2015.

Christiansen, Rupert. *Paris Babylon: The Story of the Paris Commune.* New York: Viking, 1994.

Chuzeville, Julien. *Léo Frankel: Communard sans frontières.* Paris: Editions Libertalia, 2021.

Clayson, Hollis. *Painted Love: Prostitution in French Art of the Impressionist Era.* New Haven, CT: Yale University Press, 1991.

———. *Paris in Despair: Art and Everyday Life under Siege (1870–1871).* Chicago: University of Chicago Press, 2002.

Coghlan, J. Michelle. *Sensational Internationalism: The Paris Commune and the Remapping of American Memory in the Long Nineteenth Century.* Edinburgh: Edinburgh University Press, 2016.

Cole, G.D.H. *Socialist Thought: The Forerunners, 1789–1850.* London: Macmillan, 1953.

Corbin, Alain. *Women for Hire: Prostitution and Sexuality in France after 1850.* Translated by Alan Sheridan. Cambridge, MA: Harvard University Press, 1990.

Cordillot, Michel. *Eugène Varlin, internationaliste et communard.* Paris: Spartacus, 2016.

Dalotel, Alain. *André Léo (1824–1900): La Junon de la Commune.* Chauvigny: Association des Publications Chauvinoises, 2004.

———. "La Barricade des femmes." In *La Barricade,* edited by Alain Corbin and Jean-Marie Mayeur, 341–355. Paris: Editions de la Sorbonne, 1997.

———. "Les Femmes dans les clubs rouges, 1870–1871." In *Femmes dans la cité 1815–1871,* edited by Alain Corbin, Jacqueline Lalouette, and Michèle Riot-Sarcey. Paris: Creaphis, 1997.

Dalotel, Alain, Alain Faure, and Jean-Claude Freiermuth. *Aux origines de la Commune: Le mouvement des réunions publiques à Paris 1868–1870.* Paris: Maspero, 1980.

Deluermoz, Quentin. *Commune(s) 1870–1871: Une traverse des mondes au xix siècle.* Paris: Editions du Seuil, 2020.

———. *Le Crépuscule des révolutions (1848–1871).* Paris: Éditions du Seuil, 2012.

———. "Des communardes sur les barricades." In *Penser la violence des femmes*, edited by Coline Cardi and Genevieve Pruvost, 133–150. Paris: La Découverte, 2012.

———. "Les Gamins de Paris au combat? Les enfants-soldats sous la Commune de Paris (1871)." Paper presented at L'enfant-combattant, pratiques et réprésentations, Amiens, France, November 2010.

———. "The IWMA and the Commune: A Reassessment." In *"Arise Ye Wretched of the Earth": The First International in a Global Perspective*, edited by Fabrice Bensimon, Quentin Deluermoz, and Jeanne Moisand, 107–126. Leiden: Brill, 2018.

Dineson, Wilhelm. *Paris under Communen, Paris sous la Commune*. Paris: Michel de Maule, 2003.

Dupeyron, Jean-Francois. *À l'école de la Commune de Paris: L'histoire d'une autre école*. Dijon: Editions Raison et Passions, 2020.

Duveau, Georges. *Le Siège de Paris: Septembre 1870–janvier 1871*. Paris: Hachette, 1939.

Edwards, Stewart, ed. *The Communards of Paris, 1871*. Ithaca, NY: Cornell University Press, 1973.

———. *The Paris Commune 1871*. New York: Quadrangle Books, 1971.

Eichner, Carolyn J. "Civilization vs. Solidarity: Louise Michel and the Kanak." *Salvage Quarterly* 4 (February 2017): 84–97.

———. "Language of Imperialism, Language of Liberation: Louise Michel and the Kanak-French Colonial Encounter." *Feminist Studies* 45, no. 2 (2019): 377–408.

———. *Surmounting the Barricades: Women in the Paris Commune*. Bloomington: Indiana University Press, 2004.

Farcy, Jean-Claude. "Une source inédite: Le registre des enfants de la Commune de Paris (1871)." *Criminocorpus* (September 2020). http://journals.openedition.org/criminocorpus/7417.

Fournier, Eric. *"La Commune n'est pas morte": Les usages politiques du passé, de 1871 à nos jours*. Paris: Editions Libertalia, 2013.

———. *Paris en ruines*. Paris: Editions Imago, 2008.

Galvez, Marie. "La Bibliothèque nationale et la Commune de Paris (18 mars–28 mai, 1871)." *Revue de la BnF* 2, no. 50 (2015): 70–85.

Gastaldello, Fernanda. *André Léo (1824–1900), femme écrivain au XIXe siècle*. Chauvigny: Association des publications Chauvinoises, 2001.

———. "André Léo: Quel Socialisme?" Unpublished dissertation, University of Padua. Italy, 1979.

Godineau, Laure. *La Commune de Paris par ceux qui l'ont vécu.* Paris: Parigramme, 2010.

———. "Le Retour d'exil, un nouvel exil? Le cas des communards." *Matériaux pour l'histoire de notre temps* 67 (2002): 11–16.

Gorman, Anthony. "Internationalist Thought, Local Practice: Life and Death in the Anarchist Movement in 1890s Egypt." In *The Long 1890s in Egypt: Colonial Quiescence, Subterranean Resistance,* edited by Marilyn Booth and Tony Gorman. Edinburgh: Edinburgh University Press, 2014.

Gullickson, Gay. *Unruly Women of Paris.* Ithaca, NY: Cornell University Press, 1996.

Harrison, Casey. "The Paris Commune of 1871, the Russian Revolution of 1905, and the Shifting of the Revolutionary Tradition." *History and Memory* 19, no. 2 (Fall/Winter 2007): 5–42.

Hunt, Persis. "Feminism and Anti-Clericalism under the Commune." *Massachusetts Review* 12 (Summer 1971): 418–431.

Hutton, Patrick H. *The Cult of Revolutionary Tradition: The Blanquists in French Politics, 1864–1893.* Berkeley: University of California Press, 1981.

Jellinek, Frank. *The Paris Commune of 1871.* New York: Universal Library, 1965. (First published 1937 by Victor Gollancz Ltd.)

Johnson, Martin. *The Paradise of Association: Political Culture and Popular Organizations in the Paris Commune of 1871.* Ann Arbor: University of Michigan Press, 1996.

Jones, Kathleen, and Françoise Vergès. "'Aux Citoyennes!': Women, Politics, and the Paris Commune of 1871." *History of European Ideas* 13, no. 6 (1991): 711–732.

———. "Women of the Paris Commune." *Women's Studies International Forum* 14, no. 5 (1991): 491–503.

Kerbaul, Eugène. *Nathalie Le Mel: Une Bretonne révolutionnaire et feministe.* Paris: Chez l'auteur, 1997.

Magraw, Roger. *The Age of Artisan Revolutions, 1815–1871.* Oxford: Blackwell, 1992.

Maitron, Jean. *Dictionnaire biographique du mouvement ouvrier et du mouvement social.* https://maitron.fr/spip.php?article69999, version mise en ligne le 26 juillet 2009, dernière modification le 30 juin 2020.

McMillan, James F. *France and Women 1789–1914: Gender, Society and Politics.* New York: Routledge, 2000.

Merle, Isabelle. *Expériences coloniales: La Nouvelle-Calédonie (1853–1920).* Paris: Belin, 1995.

Merriman, John. *Massacre: The Life and Death of the Paris Commune.* New York: Basic Books, 2014.

Miller, Randolph. "A New Brand of Men: Masculinity in French Republican Socialist Rhetoric." PhD dissertation, University of Wisconsin, Milwaukee, 2018.

Mordey, Delphine. "*Moments musicaux*: High Culture in the Paris Commune." *Cambridge Opera Journal* 22, no. 1 (2011): 1–31.

Moses, Claire Goldberg. *French Feminism in the Nineteenth Century.* Albany: State University of New York Press, 1984.

Moses, Claire Goldberg, and Leslie Rabine. *Feminism, Socialism, and French Romanticism.* Bloomington: Indiana University Press, 1993.

Moss, Bernard. *The Origins of the French Labor Movement 1830–1914: The Socialism of Skilled Workers.* Berkeley: University of California Press, 1976.

Mullaney, Marie Marmo. "Sexual Politics in the Career and Legend of Louise Michel." *Signs: Journal of Women in Culture and Society* 15, no. 2 (Winter 1990): 300–322.

Noiriel, Gèrard. *Une histoire Populaire de la France: De la guerre de Cent Ans à nos jours.* Marseilles: Agone, 2018.

Nye, Robert. *Masculinity and Male Codes of Honor in Modern France.* Berkeley: University of California Press, 1993.

Offen, Karen. *European Feminisms, 1700–1950.* Stanford, CA: Stanford University Press, 2000.

Plaetzer, Niklas, "Decolonizing the 'Universal Republic': The Paris Commune and French Empire." *Nineteenth-Century French Studies* 49, nos. 3–4 (Spring–Summer 2021): 585–603.

Planté, Christine. "Le Récit impossible: Malvina Blanchecotte, Tablettes d'une femme pendant la Commune." In *Ecrire la Commune: Témoignages, récits et romans (1871–1931),* edited by Roger Bellet and Philippe Régnier. Tusson: Du Lérot, 1994.

Rancière, Jacques. *The Nights of Labor: The Workers' Dream in Nineteenth-Century France.* Philadelphia: Temple University Press, 1989.

Rebérioux, Madelaine. "Le Mur des fédérés." In *Pour que vive l'histoire,* 479–500. Paris: Belin, 2017.

Redmond, René. *L'Anticléricalisme en France de 1815 à nos jours.* Paris: Fayard, 1999.

Rey, Claudine, Annie Gayat, and Sylvie Pepino. *Petit dictionnaire des femmes de la Commune: Les oubliées de l'histoire.* Paris: Editions Le bruit des autres, 2013.

Riot-Sarcey, Michèle. *Le Procès de la liberté: Une histoire souterraine du XIXe siècle en France.* Paris: La Découverte, 2016.

Roberts, J. M. "La Mémoire des vaincus: L'example de Victorine B., Souvenirs d'une morte vivante." In *Ecrire la Commune: Témoignages, récits et romans (1871–1931),* edited by Roger Bellet and Philippe Régnier. Tusson: Du Lérot, 1994.

Ross, Kristin. *Communal Luxury: The Political Imaginary of the Paris Commune.* New York: Verso, 2015.

———. *The Emergence of Social Space: Rimbaud and the Paris Commune.* London: Verso, 2008.

Rougerie, Jacques. *La Commune de 1871.* Paris: Presses Universitaires de France, 2019.

———. *Eugène Varlin: Aux origins du movement ouvrier.* Paris: Editions du Détour, 2020.

———. *Paris Libre 1871.* Paris: Editions du Seuil, 1971.

———, ed. *Procès des Communards.* Paris: René Julliard, 1964.

Sanchez, Gonzalo. *Organizing Independence: The Artists Federation of the Paris Commune and Its Legacy, 1871–1889.* Lincoln: University of Nebraska Press, 1997.

Schulkind, Eugene. *The Paris Commune of 1871.* London: Historical Association, 1871.

———. "Socialist Women during the 1871 Paris Commune." *Past and Present* 106 (February 1985): 124–163.

Scott, Joan Wallach. *Only Paradoxes to Offer: French Feminists and the Rights of Man*. Cambridge, MA: Harvard University Press, 1996.

Shafer, David. "Plus que des ambulancières: Women in Articulation and Defense of Their Ideals during the Paris Commune (1871)." *French History* 7, no. 1 (1993): 85–101.

Singer-Lecocq, Yvonne. *Rouge Elisabeth*. Paris: Editions Stock, 1977.

Soukholmine, Vassili. "Deux femmes russes combattantes de la Commune." *Cahiers Internationaux* 16 (May 1950): 53–62.

Sowerwine, Charles. *Sisters or Citizens? Women and Socialism in France since 1876*. Cambridge: Cambridge University Press, 1982.

Stovall, Tyler. *Transnational France: The Modern History of a Universal Nation*. Boulder, CO: Westview Press, 2015.

Thomas, Edith. *Louise Michel, ou La Velléda de l'anarchie*. Paris: Gallimard, 1971.

———. *Les Pétroleuses*. Paris: Gallimard, 1963.

Tomba, Massimiliano. *Insurgent Universality: An Alternative Legacy of Modernity*. New York: Oxford University Press, 2019.

Tombs, Robert. "How Bloody Was La Semaine Sanglante? A Revision." *The Historical Journal* 55, no. 3 (2012): 679–704.

Traugott, Mark. *The Insurgent Barricade*. Berkeley: University of California Press, 2010.

Varlin, Eugène. *Pratique militante et écris d'un ouvrier communard*. Edited by Paule Lejeune. Paris: Maspero, 1971.

Verhaeghe, Sidonie. "Une pensée politique de la Commune: Louise Michel à travers ses conférences." *Actuel Marx* 2, no. 66 (2019): 81–98.

———. "Les Victimes furent sans nom et sans nombre: Louise Michel et la mémoire des morts de la Commune de Paris." *Mots. Les langages du politique* 100 (2012). http://journals.openedition.org/mots/20979.

Vincent, Steven K. *Between Marxism and Anarchism: Benoît Malon and French Reformist Socialism*. Berkeley: University of California Press, 1992.

———. *Pierre-Joseph Proudhon and the Rise of French Republican Socialism*. New York: Oxford University Press, 1984.

Voici l'aube: L'immortelle Commune de Paris. Paris: Editions Sociales, 1972.

Wilson, Colette E. *Paris and the Commune 1871–78: The Politics of Forgetting.* Manchester: Manchester University Press, 2007.

Wolikow, Serge. "Les Instituteurs et la Commune." *La Nouvelle critique* (February 1971): 81–94.

Zaidman, Pierre-Henri. *Émile Duval (1840–1871), general de la Commune.* Paris: Editions Dittmar, 2006.

Index

Note: Page numbers in italics indicate figures.

About the Author

CAROLYN J. EICHNER teaches in the Departments of History and Women's and Gender Studies at the University of Wisconsin, Milwaukee. Her books include *Surmounting the Barricades: Women in the Paris Commune* and *Feminism's Empire.*

Printed and bound by CPI Group (UK) Ltd, Croydon, CR0 4YY

25/03/2025

14647325-0001